Claim Your
COMPETITVE EDGE

Attend the 3 Fun-packed Days for

Power, Passion, Prosperity, & H

RCE SYSTEM

GUEST PASS
(Valued at $1600)

To redeem your guest pass for a seat to
Claim Your Competitive Edge™ go to
CYCEdge.com/drtmb or call 778 737 2063

Claim Your
COMPETITVE EDGE™

3 Fun-packed Days for Applying the
CORE AFFLUENT SYSTEM for more

Power, Passion, Prosperity, & Purpose

* A fully refundable $7 no-show deposit required at time of registration.
See reverse for complete details.

BAR★N MASTERY INSTITUTE   CYCEdge.com/drtmb

GUEST PASS
(Valued at $1600)

To redeem your guest pass for a seat to
Claim Your Competitive Edge™ go to
CYCEdge.com/drtmb or call 778 737 2063

Claim Your
COMPETITVE EDGE™

3 Fun-packed Days for Applying the
CORE AFFLUENT SYSTEM for more

Power, Passion, Prosperity, & Purpose

* A fully refundable $7 no-show deposit required at time of registration.
See reverse for complete details.

BAR★N MASTERY INSTITUTE   CYCEdge.com/drtmb

Seating is **LIMITED** therefore allocated on a
First-Come First-Served Basis

To Reserve Your Seat GO NOW to
CYCEdge.com/drtmb

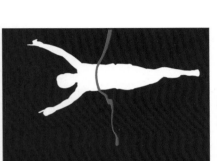

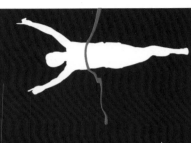

This ticket entitles the holder to one seat at the "Claim Your Competitive Edge™" event.
The value of $1600 for the event is waived however; it may not be exchanged for any other Baron Mastery Institute program or product.

The $77 fully refundable no-show deposit that is required for registration will be returned to you upon completion of the 3-day event.

To redeem your guest pass for a seat to Claim Your Competitive Edge™ go to
CYCEdge.com/drtmb or call 778 737 2063

Claim Your Competitive Edge™ is one of the most upbeat, lively, and **experiential** events you'll ever attend. The amount of **knowledge and practical tools** you'll gain **will propel you to new heights of success** in your relationships, health and finances.

"Missing out on this event is like missing the juice of life itself!"

This ticket entitles the holder to one seat at the "Claim Your Competitive Edge™" event.
The value of $1600 for the event is waived however; it may not be exchanged for any other Baron Mastery Institute program or product.

The $77 fully refundable no-show deposit that is required for registration will be returned to you upon completion of the 3-day event.

To redeem your guest pass for a seat to Claim Your Competitive Edge™ go to
CYCEdge.com/drtmb or call 778 737 2063

Claim Your Competitive Edge™ is one of the most upbeat, lively, and **experiential** events you'll ever attend. The amount of **knowledge and practical tools** you'll gain **will propel you to new heights of success** in your relationships, health and finances.

"Missing out on this event is like missing the juice of life itself!"

DON'T READ THIS...
UNLESS YOU WANT MORE MONEY!

Subconscious Tactics of the Truly Affluent

Written by Dōv Baron

Dedication

This book is dedicated to my three amazing grandchildren:
Jake, Ben, and Kendle.

May you always remember the truth of who you are—Abundant
children of the universe, who naturally stand in the flow of affluence.
Spread your wings and fly beyond the limits of your mind, dive deep
into the ocean of imagination and discover the treasure of your soul
in the eyes and hearts of everyone you'll ever meet.

Thank you for inspiring me with your playful wisdom.

List of Chapters

Acknowledgements & Gratitudes v

Foreword I

Introduction V

Chapter 1:
MONEY: Why You Don't Get What You Deserve 1
Chapter 2:
Tactics for Creating Affluence in a Financial Desert 13
Chapter 3:
I Love It. I Love It Not...Your Relationship with Money 29
Chapter 4:
Be Grateful Later, Stay Broke Now 33
Chapter 5:
I Know Exactly What I Want...Kind of 39
Chapter 6:
Both Fear and Clarity Have a Price 47
Chapter 7:
How to Dramatically Reduce Your Learning Curve 61
Chapter 8:
Are Your Friends Keeping You Broke? 67
Chapter 9:
Modeling: Don't Ask Losers How to Be Winners 75
Chapter 10:
We Don't Value What We Don't Understand 83
Chapter 11:
Money Myths 91
Chapter 12:
How Pain Can Make You Rich 101
Chapter 13:
How To Win The Lottery Without Going Bankrupt.................. 107

Chapter 14:
Beliefs: How to Use Them to Predict the Future 117
Chapter 15:
Karma Down: Who's Been Sending You Crap? 123
Chapter 16:
4 Steps to Freedom 129
Chapter 17:
The Power of Contribution in Making You Wealthy 141
Chapter 18:
Why You Can't Get Rich on Approval 151
Chapter 19:
The Power of Consequences 161
Chapter 20:
Getting Them to Bang Down Your Door to Give You Money 173
Chapter 21:
Your Unique Value Set...The Path to Infinite Riches 183
Chapter 22:
Why Helping Others Succeed Will Make You Rich 197
Chapter 23:
Your Dad's Job is Gone 203
Chapter 24:
The Ph.D. Sized Lie about How to Get Rich 207
Chapter 25:
There's Nothing Passive about Residual Income 223
Chapter 26:
The Power of Leverage 229
Chapter 27:
It's Good to be the King/Queen 247
Chapter 28:
What if You're Broke Compared to Where You Could Be? 257

About the Author 265

Tell Us What You Think 267

Declaration of Financial Independance 269

Acknowledgements
& Gratitudes

As always, my first thank you is to my beloved wife, life partner and business partner **Renuka:** *You are my muse, my greatest inspiration. Renuka works so diligently with me to bring our message to the world. Renuka, you are the light of my life, my "guru of kind." Your amazing talent for being able to do the things that others would say are impossible truly astounds me. You are without doubt one of the most talented, intelligent, funny and powerful people I have ever had the honour of knowing. You continue to inspire me. Without you, your belief and support of what we do, so many lives would go untouched. Your relentless adherence to quality control always makes me look better than I am. Thank you for your graphical design and making sure all the T's were dotted and I's were crossed. (Yes I said it that way on purpose.) Thank you, thank you, thank you!*

My thanks also go out to the many members of my spiritual family, team, friends, and associates who believe in the teachings we share and as a result have committed to getting the word out. Extra Special thanks to Alan Lary, Agustian (Gus) Hermanto, Woodeene Koenig-Bricker, Cindy Pearlman, Lee Edward Födi, Scott Paton, Stephan Stavrakis, Brian Montgomery, Arthur Samuel Joseph, John Assaraf, Peter Sage, Anurag Gupta, Nick Banks, Garry Johnson, Bret Tredwell, Vally Haeck, Naseem Rahman, Damian Loth, Barbara Madani, Anthony Madani, Scott Schilling, Peggy McCall, Judy O'Beirn and her team, Michael Mills, Eitan Sharir, Carol Aitken, Grant & Natalie Gibson, Maeve Reynolds, Steve Kiges, Terri Hawkins, Trevor "ToeCracker" Crook, Tony McAleer, Annie Hopper, John Rowley, John Drennan, Harris Abro, Capryce Mullineux, and Kathy Buckley. I'm sorry that I didn't write the names of everyone of you who have been so wonderful kind and supportive. I know I have only named a few of so many— even so—I am filled with deep and sincere gratitude.

There are several people I want to separately thank with all my heart, not just for what they do, but for who they are.

A special thank you to **Alan Lary:** *Al, your tireless conviction to be a conduit for the work that we do, the knowledge that we bring and the lives that we touch is beyond anything I could have asked for. You are a blessing in our lives. You have put yourself on the line for us so many times, and in so many ways. It has been an honour to watch the transformation from who you were to the outstanding example of an ever growing ever developing spectacular human being. You are the living example of what is possible for those who are willing to do what it takes to go beyond their conditioning. Thank you is clearly inadequate; I have no words that can adequately convey my sincere gratitude, except to say, "I love you."*

Lee Edward Födi: *Lee, you are my 'go-to guy': Your all-around freakin amazing skills have saved my rear end way too many times. Above all, you are one of the most courageous men I know—a true friend and a brother. Thank you!*

Vally Haeck: *So many lives have been touched and changed by who 'you are' and 'what you do.' I know you like to stay off center stage; however, you are center stage in my respect and love. Working with us you always went above and beyond the call of duty. Thanks to you, your amazing work ethic, and your superior commitment, there are many people around the world whose lives have been shifted through our work. You were the one who took our work to the electronic world. Your commitment to doing what it takes to make sure everyone who can possibly get on-line, find out about who we are and what we do, has transformed many more lives than any of us will ever know. Thank you!*

Agustian (Gus) Hermanto: *Gussy, I can still clearly remember the shy human resources guy who came for the interview. How wonderful it has been to watch you blossom into a powerful, dynamic, emotionally connected guy with a massive bag of tricks. Gus I am so grateful to have you as part of our team. Your willingness to learn, your commitment to finding a solution for whatever the challenge, your infinite patience, and your passion are truly inspirational. It is such a wonderful blessing to have someone with your level of integrity standing by our side in all manner of circumstances and situations. I deeply love and respect you.*

My sincere gratitude to all the members of the Baron Mastery Institute Team, official or otherwise: *I want all of you to know how grateful I am to each and every one of you. A special thank you to all the BMI Ambassadors, who walk your talk, live these teachings, and share your success stories with us and the world. You rock!*

Thanks would be incomplete without acknowledging my outstanding editor **Woodeene Koenig-Bricker**. *Thank you for managing to keep my voice in every word and on every page while still cleaning up my grammatical mess. Thank you for your belief in and enthusiasm for this project. It's been both a pleasure and an honour working with you.*

Later in this book I'll be speaking extensively on leverage. For this very subject I want to offer my sincere gratitude to **Scott Paton**. *Scott, you twisted my arm into doing podcasts and thanks to your commitment and ability to leverage iTunes, within one year over a hundred thousand people around the world were tuned into: FreeMindMasteryPodcast.com. Thanks for showing up week after week to be "the other bloke talking about interesting stuff," and creating a new way for us to raise consciousness and have positive impact.*

These acknowledgements would also be incomplete without my sincere gratitude for **John Assaraf**—a man who is a clear example of wealth by being the magnifying glass that just makes who you are more obvious. John's integrity, wisdom, kindness and generosity have only grown as he has become more successful. I am honoured to call John both a mentor and a friend.

The other half of the editorial team is the wordsmith, eagle eyed **Cindy Pearlman**. *Thank you for jumping in at the last minute.*

Finally, I would like to thank you and all my students around the world—past, present and future—for your inquiring minds, warm hearts, and bright courageous souls. Each one of you lifts my life to progressively higher levels.

With sincere gratitude, Dov...

Foreword

As I read this book I couldn't help but think of how many people just don't understand why they don't have money or, if they do, it's really not in abundance. Most people live their lives in quiet desperation wishing and wanting more money, yet never really learning anything at all about themselves or making more of that green stuff with ink on it that we refer to as money.

In the old days, gold, pigs, cows, chocolate, and many other forms of exchange were used to represent money. Many people were taught that if you worked hard you could earn a living and take care of yourself and your family. If you were lucky and made some wise investments, maybe you could even retire and not work anymore.

Then, as time passed and education was seen as the way to earn money, the order of the day was go to school, get a degree, and work hard for some big company so they would take care of you during your career and hopefully during retirement. Well, we all know that this was a recipe for disaster and it blew up in the faces of millions who believed it.

I share this reflection with you because within your hands is the truth—the truth about you and the truth about you and money. The question is: Can you handle the truth? Can you accept the responsibility of earning it, investing it and saving it? Can you accept that you and only you, can decide and then learn, how to think about money in a unique and different way, and then acquire it easier, faster and with more fun than ever before?

I

If you answered *yes* to any or all these questions, I believe that you are ready to become wealthy in more ways than one.

Becoming wealthy is an inside out game and not an outside in game. As you will learn in the pages you hold, you must first accept the fact that you are already wealthy and a victor not a victim.

You and I are always at cause and not at effect. If this sounds a little out there and weird, all I ask is for your patience. Trust me that you will be able to understand more as you read this book. Just to give you a little hint imagine this: When you watch a movie on your TV or at a theatre, all you are seeing is whatever is being broadcast from the TV station or projected onto the screen at the theatre off a DVD. If you don't like the movie (or your life's financial results) don't blame the TV or the DVD. Just learn how to change the internal program that is broadcasting the show.

This book will teach you to think and feel differently about yourself and money. Dōv's thinking and teachings will alter your personal relationship with money and will put you totally in charge of your financial earning ability starting today.

There are so many mind-blowing ideas in this book; you really have to be ready for a paradigm shift to grasp its richness.

Some potentially very complex ideas have been broken down into simple terms anyone can grasp and apply immediately to enrich their bank account and life.

I personally love a book that will challenge me intellectually, and at the same time lead me to some big aha's that can transform my mind and finances, and this book does both.

Dōv has once again created a masterpiece that will have people talking about money in ways it has rarely, if ever, been discussed.

You now hold within your hands the secret to your financial success.

John Assaraf
New York Times Bestselling Author,
"The Answer" and "Having It All."
Featured in The blockbuster movie
and book "The Secret."
CEO, OneCoach

Introduction

Each Ending is a New Beginning

The years immediately preceding 2008 were politically turbulent ones. The United States and many other countries were actively involved in two major wars and several smaller ones. The threat of terrorism had become media normality and the housing market had gone nuts. Nonetheless, money was flowing, there were lots of jobs, and the Internet was booming. Despite insane gas prices and greater evidence of global warming, cash was flowing and people were still buying bigger and bigger homes, Gucci bags, and gigantic SUVs. The economic theme song could easily have been made famous by the Beatles: "Money...that's what I want."

Then in the late summer of 2008, there came a whispering of something many refused to hear. Many went out and borrowed more in hopes of buying even at a high price because they were sure it would get higher. Suddenly, at least for those who refused to see the signs, the economic airbus crashed into the mountain of hope. A wave of economic devastation that would potentially collapse the global economy began to drown us.

A tsunami of fear flooded the globe and jobs disappeared under the surge. Homes were foreclosed. Banks went under and long established old money companies went bankrupt or needed the government to bail them out.

Was it all over? Would business recover? Was this some kind of an apocalyptic warning that the end was near? These were questions spoken about on the news, late night talk shows and in living rooms around the world.

As I write this book, it's more than a year ago since it was made official that we were in a global recession. Although bankruptcies were up by an unprecedented 34.6 percent over the first quarter of 2009, a subtle but growing sense of hope is returning. This hope is not for things to return to the way they were although there are many who would want it that way. The growing hope seems to be for a growing "healthy economy," based more on collaboration that direct and adversarial completion.

The world and its economics have changed and I don't believe it can ever be the same. The belief in a stable job has buckled at the knees. The corporate ladder has been pushed over. The result is that many people are less willing to be dependent on some outside force for their financial certainty. In many ways, it is that quiet rumbling within the middle class mind that has catalyzed this book into reality.

Yes, the economy has changed. However, the opportunity to live the life of your dreams did not die with the announcement of a recession. There have been many recessions, 14 since the "Great Depression" of 1929 and although people thought some of them were going to be financially fatal, in the long run that was never an actuality.

In this new economy we will have to do things differently, and this book is dedicated to you discovering how you can not only survive but flourish by tapping into what you have that no one else has—even if you don't know what that is—yet.

So let's use this ending as a new beginning. For many of you, these pages are our first meeting…Hello, I'm Dōv Baron. Nice to meet you and thank you for trusting me enough to invest in this book. It's highly likely that before you picked up this book you may never have even heard of me. This is the beginning of what I trust will be an expanding relationship. I've been teaching workshops and seminars around the world since the mid-eighties to a very wide range of folks, many of whom I'm sure are just like you—individuals who are hungry for a bigger experience of life, not just in financial terms but also in the areas of life that are more than just money. Even though I have been a student of human development and have taught workshops and seminars on a wide variety of subjects pertaining to the human condition and how to reach higher and higher levels of excellence, I don't claim to have all the answers. No one does and they lie if they say they do. What I do have is a proven track record for making very complex psychological, metaphysical and even quantum principles easy to both understand and apply.

According to those who have worked with me over the years, I have a very specific style of delivery. It's one that cuts through the crap. (Yes, I've even been known to use the occasional expletive.) It gives you what you need, not necessarily what you "think" you want. So be warned that if you like your personal development served on a bed of clouds dressed in rainbows that's not what you're likely to find here. What you will find is to the point, practical knowledge and tools you can begin using before you are even close to finishing reading this book.

One more thing. Much of this book is dedicated to assisting you in the process of tapping into and claiming your unique value. As I will clearly explain, the ego-mind is going to be looking for reasons to not take in anything that challenges what "it" has held as "true." (Note small "t".)

One of the ways the ego-mind does this is by distracting and confusing you, pulling you off into some kind of mind meander. Sometimes that means focusing on "stuff" rather than taking in what's right in front of you. If, at any time, you find yourself becoming spontaneously confused, tired, or thinking about "stuff" that just doesn't matter, be warned. That's your ego-mind trying to pull you away from a part of the material that could have profound meaning for you. In order to assist you with this, you will find that I write in a very conversational style. You may be able to hear my voice in your head rather than read text on a page. Something else that will help is throughout the book you will likely notice the occasional spelling mistake or what you could consider a grammatical error. They might be there on purpose. The ego-mind loves doing the perfectionist thing in order to delay or just avoid. Your job is to notice that your ego-mind is noticing these things and then quickly move on.

Throughout this book are many case studies of individuals, some of whom may seem to be "you." There's a good chance that the person being referred to is not you. However, please be aware that for obvious reasons, unless otherwise stated, the names and sometimes even the gender of the person being referred to has been changed. As you continue reading, you will discover with all certainty that your life is, with or without your knowing, on purpose. What you are about to discover is whether it is on purpose that you stay broke or on purpose that you experience being in the flow of affluent abundance.

Chapter 1

MONEY: Why You Don't Get What You Deserve

Why is it that the media and other breeders of doom and gloom keep telling us, "There's no money!" Is that possibly true?

I mean, come on, think about it.

Of course, it's not true. Money didn't get up one Sunday morning, watch CNN, and upon hearing someone say there was a recession merely evaporated, did it? Money simply moves from one place to another. All the money that was ever there is still there. In fact, according to one of my favorite metaphysical teachers Stuart Wilde, money is always multiplying. The message that there is a limited supply of the green stuff and every time some of it goes out, there is less for you or someone else in the world, is actually a lie. The truth is that money is simply in a constant state of flow. Actually, those who really understand that concept make a lot of it in a "down market." They understand that affluence is all about flow. In fact the word affluence comes from the Latin and old French meaning "to flow." I'll take you deeper into the understanding of affluence as we get deeper into this book.

1

Now, let me say right off the bat that I know that money seems real; in fact, as you may have observed, it seems most real when you don't have it. Have you noticed when people "have" money they also have a tendency to pick up the tab and put it on a credit card without really thinking? But, when the budget gets tight, money becomes very real and people can have a tendency to "watch" every penny. There is something that's astounding, and I promise I'll prove everything I'm about to say, even if it seems outrageous or a little wacky. First, I want you to allow your mind to grasp hold of this thought for a moment: Money is nothing more than an idea.

Let me say it again: *Money is nothing more than an idea.*

I know, it sounds crazy, like someone sitting around in long white robes passing on a message from a disembodied spirit living on another plane. But it's not! What's more, I'll prove it to you by taking you on a little journey through the recent history of money as we know it and how it works.

Our journey begins a little more than 300 years ago, in 1694, when the first Bank of England initiated something called "fractional reserve banking." (You can research this, and it's fascinating.) What "fractional reserve banking" meant is that for every dollar you deposited into the bank or loaned from the bank, the institution had the right to create another ten dollars. (I told you it was fascinating.) That meant and means—because they are still doing it today—is that money is created out of thin air.

Now, you should also know that this practice became such a bone of contention with the American people that Benjamin Franklin said it was one of the main reasons for the War of Independence. Franklin and the Founding Fathers wanted America to have nothing to do with "fractional reserve banking." They wanted America's money kept in the hands of the American people because Franklin and the others wanted Americans to have that independence.

Just to give you an idea of how opposed the new American leaders were to this system, take a look at this:

> *I believe that banking institutions are more dangerous*
> *to our liberties than standing armies.*
> *The issuing power should be taken from the banks and*
> *restored to the people to whom it properly belongs.*
>
> *~President Thomas Jefferson*

Jumping ahead, in 1913 the 28th President of the United States, Woodrow Wilson signed a document called the *Federal Reserve* Act that essentially put that money back in the hands of the bankers.

Now here's where it starts to get really intriguing because you will begin to see that money is in fact not real.

But wait, I'm getting ahead of myself. Let's go back to history.

Once the *Federal Reserve* Act was in place, these bankers had the ability to create money based on your signature. (Again, you can go do the research on this; it's absolutely true.) What that means in the most basic form is that your signature has value and the bankers know it even if you don't. You see, they understand you have worth just by virtue of your signature. I wonder if you know that? I wonder if you really understand that you actually have an intrinsic worth?

It's a worth that's not based on money in your bank account, your car or your house, or any other material thing.

Are you now beginning to understand that money is created from an idea? When that idea gets strong enough, something miraculous happens. You'll start to understand what I mean by that in a little while.

Now I want us to begin to look at why more than 90 percent of people never achieve financial independence and what you can do to make sure you don't become part of that statistic, but actually reach financial independence by being in the flow of affluence.

So, let's dive right in. How can you get in that flow? Something I like to tell people is:

*"In life you don't get what you deserve;
you get what you believe you deserve."*

~Dõv Baron

What that means is the idea or belief you have about your worth will end up determining your bank account. This is why bad things happen to good people and real "douche bags" seem to have good fortune. This part may be a bit of a stretch for you, but I promise that I'll back it all up with science later. For now I would like for you to consider that all the situations and circumstances we find ourselves in come from something I call *Unconscious Deserving*.

Our Unconscious Deserving is held in place by a set of beliefs that you have accepted without question up until now. This set of beliefs tells us our worth and, as such, what we deserve. Now before you jump to any conclusions, you should know, for the most part, this is all going on unconsciously and all too often doesn't make any sense to the conscious mind. Nonetheless, whatever it is that we unconsciously believe we deserve is what is being fed directly out into the quantum field. (We'll take a good look at this later in the book.) Now, what's great is that when you begin questioning even your conscious beliefs, you are inadvertently questioning your level of unconscious deserving. As a result, you begin changing or at least shaking the foundations of what has been your unconscious deserving. By doing that, what starts showing up in your life is very different from what has been your usual fare.

So Where Are We?

As you might have guessed, what all this means is your wealth is based on your self-worth, which is why so few people ever achieve financial independence. They either devalue or just don't recognize their worth. Now if your bank account is a reflection of the level of self-worth someone holds, the natural question might be, "Why would anyone do that to themselves?"

Well, let's take a look. First of all, they lack the belief. This could be in themselves, but it could just as easily be in the possibility of "it" happening for them. As you will see when you get deeper into this book, a belief is a series of "facts" that you have collected. However, please note that **just because we call something a fact doesn't make it one**. In truth, we make "facts" up all the time. For instance there are cultures in the world today that still hold it as a "fact" that a woman can never be of as much value as a man. Even today in India, a country with one of the fastest growing economies in the world, there is still a caste system that holds it as a "fact" that some people, by virtue of their bloodline, are dirty or "untouchable." Some cultures hold as a "fact" that people born with darker skin are of a lower value. If you doubt what I'm saying, you may want to travel in Asia where they sell skin-lightening products in pharmacies and every little general store. All this is going on while here in the Western world we like to hold it as "a fact" that the news is always true and that women have equal rights to men. Like I said, we make up "facts" all the time.

What I shared a few pages back was the understanding that money is created out of an idea. Therefore, may I suggest that you begin to focus on that in order to develop the belief that you can get in the flow of affluence and become financially independent.

Another reason people do not achieve financial independence is they do not have rock solid outcomes they are moving towards. They have vague ideas, but nothing concrete on which to focus. They aren't focused on where they are going, and most often they aren't even focused on where they are. Most people who are financially struggling are looking back to where they've been or ahead to potential problems rather than seeing where they could actually be.

The third thing that stops people from getting financial independence is, well you probably guessed it: Fear. F – E – A – R—False Evidence Appearing Real. People focus on that fear with a life or death intent. If they just applied that level of focus and intention to achieving the life of their dreams, they would not be financially struggling any longer. Unfortunately, we are bombarded with fear by the media. The media are constantly telling us why we cannot achieve financial independence.

The fourth reason many people do not own their true worth and reach their financial potential is they lack courage. They lack the courage to make the decisions to do what it takes to get to their financial destination. You have got to be able to make those decisions that others fear to make. It takes courage to own your worth in the face of others who would tell you your worth is less than it is.

Here's what you will truly want to comprehend: The most successful people in the world in any economic situation are the people who are making the decisions. Take a look around. The decision makers are the ones who are not only doing well in any economy, but they are the ones who are flourishing. They make decisions about opportunities that others cannot even see because those other people are blinded by their own fears.

Now that you understand that your wealth is directly associated to your self-worth, I want to really clarify this point for you. I want you to get this at the deepest possible level, because once you do, you will claim your value and you will never let anyone take it from you again.

I would love to show you a video clip from my Equation for Manifestation Home Study program that really demonstrates what I'm talking about, however, as this is a traditional book, that's not going to happen. So here's what I want you to do. Imagine that you are in the audience at one of my live events. You've been chatting to the people around you and you can see their faces lighting up. You are excited about all the amazing things you are learning and you feel transformed by the information. You are enthralled to see what happens next.

You see me standing center stage and hear me begin by stating, "I would like to talk to you about something that I believe is an extraordinarily important subject because it so often gets missed. We live in a culture and a time where there has been a big emphasis on building our self-esteem. And although that is somewhat good, with this emphasis, one of the major factors that is affecting your level of wealth and success in a general sense is getting overlooked. The root of your financial results is not your self-esteem, but rather your level of self-worth."

At this point, you become very curious, because well, quite simply all of us have been led to believe that great self-esteem is in fact the key to the kingdom. You listen as I continue, "Here's what the research shows about self-worth. Your level of real success is always equal to your level of self-worth. However, your level of self-worth is equal to your level of self knowledge and your level of self knowledge is equal to your level of self development."

You look around at your fellow audience members, some of whom appear a little puzzled.

"To tie all that together, the more you know yourself and the more you develop yourself, the better your self-worth becomes. As a result, your worth increases because your wealth is determined by your worth. The challenge is that all too often we have given our self-worth to the hands of others via self-esteem."

Let me explain. We let other people determine who we are. We listen to those messages that may not be aligned with who we really are and, in the process, we begin to devalue ourselves. When you think about it, what is it that we have that is valuable or not valuable because somebody else decided it? When they put you down and said to you, "It's not going to happen for you," you got shattered from that. That was because your self-worth is being dominated by your self-esteem.

So you ask, if not out loud at least in your mind, "What is the difference between self-esteem and self-worth?" It's a great question because most people think that they are simply two ways of saying the same thing. Don't be fooled. There's a vast difference and when you get it, your wealth and finances will change for the better.

Let's nail it down. Self-esteem is external while self-worth is internal. Your self-worth is determined by how you feel about the way you bring value to the world. Self-worth is what you know about yourself at an intrinsic value level; it's what is within you.

Unless you are willing to open up and begin to embrace the gifts that were given to you when you came to this planet, even though they may have been hidden from you for a very long time, you can never really know your true worth. If we don't recognize our own value, we simply allow our self-worth to be determined by others.

Much of this book is dedicated to you discovering and tapping into your unique value because from there you will have the opportunity to reclaim your self-worth and put yourself back in the flow of affluence. Listen, I know stuff has happened in your life and I know you are not very proud of some of it. What I want to tell you from the bottom of my heart is even though you may have had times of feeling worthless, your value cannot and will not be changed by anything outside of yourself. It's what you know about yourself at an intrinsic value level that determines your self-worth.

Okay, let's go back to you being at the live event. You see me reach into my pocket and bring out a nice crisp "$100 bill." I say to you and the other members of the audience, "What is this?" You reply, "A hundred dollar bill."

I hold it up and ask you, "If I take this into the bank, what will they tell me it's worth?"

You and your fellow attendees reply in unison, "One hundred dollars."

I continue, "How much is it worth at a candy store, hardware store, or a restaurant?"

Of course you shout, "One hundred dollars!"

"Hmmm, so it's worth the same where ever I take it? Well what about now?" With that I crumple up the bill in my hand. Once again I ask, "What's it worth now?" You feel a bit confused because the answer is as obvious as it has been each time I've asked the question. "One hundred dollars," you say even more firmly.

"All right, but what about now?" This time I throw the money on the floor, stomp on it, then pick it up and hurl insults at it about how it's not good enough. I tell it that it's a complete disappointment to me. I say that I thought it would turn out better than this crumpled mess. I tell it that it's ugly and stupid. And once again, I ask, "What's it worth now?"

Feeling even more confused, you say out loud one more time, "One hundred dollars!"

"How can that be? Surely, after everything it's been through, the hard times, the abuse, surely its value has gone down? Surely, it's no longer worth what it was originally?"

Suddenly you get it.

The truth is that just like this hundred dollar bill, you may have been crushed, you may have been stomped on, and you may have been abused, but your value is unchangeable. No matter what has happened to you, you are still valuable. Your self-worth is intrinsic. It is the truth of who you are. Don't let anybody take it away. Because in truth, you are a magnificent being with amazing gifts and the world will only be a better place when you are willing to know your true value isn't about what you have experienced, but who you really are at an intrinsic level.

Never give your value to somebody else, especially someone who is looking to devalue you.

The bottom line:
Shit happens. It doesn't mean that you're shit!

Does that make senses? Yes, I know I said "senses" rather than sense. The reason is simple and vastly important: When you really get something, it goes deeper than merely making logical or rational sense. When we really "get it", we feel it. Something changes within us. Sometimes there is a sudden silence in what had been a busy head; sometimes the information literally hits us in the gut. Some people begin to sweat when the material is revealed to them. Bottom line: When you really get it, it hits more than one sense and it makes senses.

Chapter 2

Tactics for Creating Affluence in a Financial Desert

Doubtlessly we live in challenging times. The markets are down then they're up; old name companies are going under and many jobs are going, too. That being said, the question becomes: Is this new? The answer is obvious: No, this is not new!

As a kid growing up in the UK, I can clearly remember several recessions including the three-day week, when power was turned on only for specific days of each week. I can remember the gasoline line-ups (petrol rationing) of the 1970s. The country was, and I quote, "Grinding to a halt." However, that wasn't true then, it isn't true now, and it only appears true as long as that is what we are fixated on.

If you keep letting all that crap into your head about there being no money available, I can guarantee that your life is not going to be the picture of abundance. To put it into the simplest of terms—if you want to experience the flow of affluence, wealth and abundance, you have to put your focus on wealth and abundance.

In the words of Qui-Gon Jinn to Anakin Skywalker in Star Wars®, "Always remember, your focus determines your reality."

With all that's going on, it's easy to lose our grounding in the most basic of facts: We live in an abundant world! Everything about the planet is abundant. If you doubt what I'm saying, go to the store and buy a papaya, pomegranate, or any other kind of fruit. What you will find is that this one fruit that grew from one tree or bush contains enough seeds to grow another 10, 50, 100 trees or bushes that in turn will produce another 10, 50, or 100 pieces of fruit. The cycle just continues to repeat. As an Earthling, abundance is your birthright. But the question for many people is how to access that birthright.

Everything in quantum physics is now proving what ancient spiritual teachings have shared for millennia: We are all connected, not just to each other but to all things. To give it to you on the nose, that means you are also connected to all the money in the world. Quantum physics shows us that everything is energy. Even the seemly solid matter of the walls that surround us and the floor beneath us ultimately is nothing more than vibrating, oscillating, energy. All of us are energy and the money you have been desirous of is, at its basic form, energy. The real secret to what allows that energy to flow to and from us is feeling. The feeling of abundance, wealth, success and being in the flow are all directly "in phase" (have a frequency match) with money and wealth being attracted to you. If you are looking at money as being scarce or even evil, you cannot be "in phase" with money flowing to you.

Money and wealth "appear" to be something that takes place in the outer world but what you will want to understand at the depth of your being is ...

Money and Wealth are an Inner Game.

If you've been financially struggling in the last little while, and many people have, you may be thinking, "Yeah, this abundant world stuff is all very nice "in theory", but the bottom line is I can't see that abundance in my bank account, so as far as I'm concerned, it's... 'whatever.'"

Let's face it. When you can't see it, it's pretty hard to believe that abundance is even possible. And if you've been financially challenged for more than a little while, it can feel like you're in a financial desert, right?

Actually let's take a look at that...Have you ever been to the desert? Get there in the middle of summer; the ground is cracked and dry and if there is a breeze, it is a hot one that whips up the top layer of what was soil and turns it into a burning dust. Sometimes in the desert literally years can go by between rainfalls. Can you imagine how dried up and lifeless the desert appears after two, three, five years without rain? Having been to the desert in the summer I can tell you that when I looked out across this bare environment and was told that in the spring, there would be an abundance of flowers, it seemed as unrealistic as a person looking at their empty bank account and trying to believe that there would be an abundance of funds filling it soon.

Fact is, I went back to the desert in spring, and it was breathtaking! What had been dried up lifeless dust just months before now flourished with streams and a carpet of the most magnificent colored flowers as far as the eye could see. On my previous visit, I had seen a tree and had been curious about how long it had been dead. This time, the tree had been miraculously transformed as if the metaphorical hand of God had reached down from heaven and brought it back to life; leaves glistening with dew seemed to wink at me between beautiful, soft-petaled blooms. It was out of this world! If it weren't for its precise location, I would not have believed I was looking at the same tree.

Standing in the desert on a hot summer's day it can be hard to believe that the temperature will get down towards freezing at night, streams will flow, flowers will bloom, and life in so many forms will wash across what looks like a lifeless environment. Even so, all these things do happen, and they happen all the time. The desert, like you, is filled with limitless potentiality for that abundance, which given the right circumstances results in the ground becoming an overflowing wealth.

My question to you is this: What magnificent abundance, what glorious affluence waits within you? What massive level of success is waiting to show up given just the right circumstances?

Now I know many people tell themselves that money doesn't matter; it's not part of their spiritual journey. I have two words for that. One starts with "B" and the other with "S." That kind of nonsense is a chicken way of avoiding the issues a person has around money. Money is not, and never will be the solution to all your problems. However, money is also not the source of everything that's wrong in the world. Let's face it, in the physical sense, money is nothing more than faces and numbers on bits of paper/cloth. We have both personally and collectively given money the meaning we have given it, and the bottom line is, as a free willed human being, you get to decide on a new meaning if you want to change your mindset.

Can I be totally honest with you? I do hope so. You see I had a bit of an internal battle about putting what you are about to read next. The reason being is that it's from one of my other books. The battle was because I wanted this book to be totally fresh. However, after some serious consideration I decided to include it here because I had to ask myself what was more important—keeping this entire book fresh, (which is good for my ego-mind) or giving you what you need in order to create breakthroughs for you in your financial world. The latter won. What follows is an excerpt from my book "Don't Read This… Your Ego Won't Like It!"

Show me the moneeeeeeeeeeey!

Your Financial Foundation
One of the first questions I hear in my seminars when I bring up the subject of having a strong financial foundation is this, "What has my mind got to do with my bank account, outside of the fact that I can use my mind to get an education in hopes of getting a better job?"

Well, this is partially correct. Using your mind to make the decision to get an education *might* land you a better job. Then again, if your ego-mind is filled with negative beliefs that, for instance, block you from believing in yourself and what you are truly capable of and deserve, that will absolutely affect your financial situation in a negative way. Because if you don't honestly believe in yourself, all the education in the world won't do you a lick of good.

A word of caution: If you don't believe in yourself and realize you're capable of amazing things, then you will either not be able to use that education, or you will never feel like you've got enough of the "right stuff."

Here are a few short examples of some internal dialogue statements and/ or beliefs that people who do not fully believe in themselves and/or are not the master of their financial ego-mind have. And once again, pay close attention to any feelings of familiarity while reading these examples because, in this case, those feelings of familiarity are big fat red flags waving around in front of you are telling you that you are outside of the flow of affluence.

These include:

- Any general unending *sense of anxiety* about money.

- Sometimes, when the subject of money is brought up, you become *tense or frustrated.*

- "Money doesn't grow on trees."

- "Rich people are selfish."

- "Rich people aren't any happier than anyone else."

- Or, maybe there's this fear that *there's just not enough of it.*

- And then, even when there is enough, you get that sneaking suspicion that *it's never going to last.*

That last example really hits so many people deep in the pit of their stomach because it's such a common misplaced belief so many people share.

One point I can't stress enough is that understanding where your beliefs about finances come from allows you to *let go* of any anxiety and frustration you may have had about money.

What truly causes excitement in me—and should always cause shivers of excitement to tingle up and down your spine—is that mastering your ego-mind gets rid of that feeling of "not enough."

Mastering the foundation of financial success grants you the freedom to live with a natural sense of abundance. This is because you will have a sense that you have the money to do the things in your life that seemed just out of reach a little while ago, because you believe in yourself and what you are capable of—even if no one else does.

Face it, money is so much more than official notes printed on paper with pictures and numbers. Money, or for that matter financial wealth, is a set of beliefs and these beliefs are a state of mind, or as you will come to understand, a *resonance* (the Law of Resonance will make more sense to you further on in this book when it's fully explained).

This is one of the six foundations of life, and if you are interested in discovering more about the other five, you can take a look at one of my other books: "Don't Read This...Your Ego Won't Like It!"

One of the most common and most limiting myths about having the life you want is that it is more spiritual to be poor than rich. I genuinely believe you can be wealthy and spiritual, but then again, you can be poor and spiritual. It's simply a matter of choice. However, owning your power to have either is not the same as settling for poverty because it's the "good" excuse. By the way, if you think poor people are inherently more spiritual let me fill you in: I grew up in a ghetto; poverty was rife, and although there were some wonderful loving and even the occasional spiritual people around, the people who we might judge as being less than spiritual were definitely in the majority. Poor people are no less or more spiritual than rich people, but what I can tell you from first hand observation is that when someone doesn't have enough money to survive, they stand a much greater chance of doing the kinds of things that we don't usually think of as good or spiritual.

Remember, money is not pure evil, money is not pure good, money is neural. Money is nothing without our using it for whatever outcome we decide upon. One more thing about wealth and poverty. Check your Bible, King Solomon was the richest king to have ever lived and according to the Old Testament, God seemed to like him well enough.

And while we are at it, "Money is not the root of all evil." Again, check your Bible. What it actually says is that, "The LOVE of money is the root of all evil." Big difference, isn't it?

Building a healthy relationship with money can be the difference between greater levels of what you do want as opposed to what you don't want, greater levels of being who you want to be as opposed to who you don't want to be. Just take a breath and for a moment think about this: At the end of your life, with all its challenges, triumphs, pain and beauty, the life you will be reviewing will be nothing more than a collection of moments that either brought you pain or joy, struggle or ease, isolation or connection, fear or love.

Not owning our power to create an abundant flow of funds is a great way to abdicate responsibility. However, those who decide to step up and own their power see personal and even collective responsibility as a spiritual act that allows them the freedom to become more of who they truly are. However, for that to happen we need to have courage. For most people, accepting responsibility is quite uncomfortable and scares the crap out of them. Nonetheless, it's the only solution to the challenges we face today, not only as individuals, but as a planet. Expecting someone else to fix our problems is childish. When you own your power, you realize you have access to all the resources you will ever need.

The difference between those who are financially poor and those who are financially abundant is so often nothing more than a subtle shift in both consciousness and enthusiasm. We live in a three-dimensional reflected universe whether we are aware of it or not. What that means is that everything that surrounds us is nothing more than a reflection of the thoughts, feelings and beliefs we have and have had about the reality we are experiencing.

Now stop for a minute, and reread that last sentence. If you can allow yourself to "get it" from this moment forward, what you experience will not only change, but so will the meaning of what you are experiencing.

Here's another thought that I believe will assist you in taking this a little deeper:

"You do not live in the world. You live in a mirror that reflects back to you who and what you are, both at a conscious and unconscious level."

Let's pretend you've had some challenges around creating financial abundance, okay? May I suggest that you start out by at least questioning if what you believe about money is actually true. I mean if you have a belief that money is hard to come by, is that really true? Or is that a conclusion you have come to using a limited amount of knowledge?

Let me explain. Go outside and look up at the sky (it doesn't matter if it's sunny or cloudy). What color is the sky? If it's cloudy, what color is the sky behind the clouds? It's blue, right? Does it matter if you believe that it's blue? Does your belief make the sky blue? Of course not. The sky is blue because molecules in the air scatter blue light from the sun more than they scatter red light. You can believe the sky is green if you want, but that doesn't make it true. The sky will always be blue no matter what you believe.

That, my friend, is the only way to actually know for sure if something is really true. If "it" (whatever you believe) remains true with or without your opinion, then there's a good chance it is actually true. Therefore, a good place to start is by reminding yourself that despite the apparent lack in your circumstances, *there's tons of money* around, at all times. I'd like you to get curious about what would happen if you began each day thinking just how much money is floating around this planet in any given day...no, forget each day, how about in each minute. Some estimates say that there is as much as six trillion dollars in circulation each minute in the United States alone. (Do you have any idea just how much a trillion is? If you spent a dollar per second, it would take you 32,000 years to spend a trillion dollars!) The fact is that there is an untold amount of money floating past and through you in any given moment. In truth, it is way more money than you could ever spend, even if spending was twelve hours a day full-time job.

Trillions and trillions of dollars are being sent through cyberspace every single day and just like radio and TV waves, all the digital money is passing right through you. Every cell of your body has been a multi millionaire before it fell away from your body.

If you've read any of my other books, eBooks, blogs, or been through my audios and videos, you know that I've been heavily into the quantum understanding of reality for more than 20 years. What's fascinating is that when you think about it, this supposedly solid reality by which we define whether we are abundant or not isn't actually solid at all. Everything exists as nothing more than a range of frequencies that you are either resonating with, in harmony with or not. According to quantum physics, this frequency isn't even set. It is in what's called a hazy wave form until it is observed. Once observed, that which was a hazy wave becomes that which we call physical reality.

That might be hard to visualize, so let me create a picture for you. Imagine floating around in a big beautiful ocean. You feel completely safe. Nothing about the water is scary; breathing is easy and everything around you also seems to flow through you, yet you have a sense that you are both somehow separate from the ocean and at the same time part of it. That's how it is for us; we are part of something called the quantum field or the zero point field. We have a sense that we are somehow separate from it, but at the same time part of it. The field contains absolutely everything in a state known as infinite possibility. What this means is that in the field anything is possible and anything can be created from that possibility. However, when we direct our consciousness with a specific intent towards the field, that state of infinite possibility (hazy wave form) collapses into a single possibility that is determined by the intent. This is known in quantum physics as "collapsing the wave form." It is our directed consciousness that creates everything in our reality from the infinite possibility that is the quantum field.

Money/affluence follows much of the same path as the law of quantum physics. In order for you to experience more money and affluence in your life, it has to move from the hazy wave form of an idea, wish, or dream, into the solid state of money in your wallet or bank account. What this means is that lack also starts out as a hazy wave form of an idea. Therefore, it is of the utmost importance that you become in sync with and centered on paying attention to the solid reality of abundance that surrounds you. When noticing those three dimensional reflections of abundance, which could come in the form of cash in your pocket, goods that surround you, even the massive amount of seeds in a tomato or anything else that seems to be the solid form of abundance, put yourself in sync or as I will refer to it later, in resonance with them by allowing yourself to not just see but also feel that abundance is around you at every turn. Now put into your mind and body with enthusiasm the "knowing" that there is more than enough money in the world for us all to live well. As you let yourself soak in the abundance that surrounds you, this knowing becomes a way for you to now accept and collect your natural birthright of abundance, because in that moment, you are in a state of affluence.

To begin to get in-phase with and in resonance with wealth and abundance, start out by putting your focus on things that you see as direct manifestation of that wealth and abundance. Put yourself in situations and environments where wealthy people hang out. It will not serve you to look at wealthy people or situations that reflect abundance with the eyes of anger or envy. These feelings simply throw you out of resonance with wealth and abundance and instead place you in resonance with lack and struggle, blocking your affluence and, as a result, causing you to attract more of that lack and struggle. If you see a person in a beautiful car or wearing beautiful clothes or jewelry, and you find yourself thinking or feeling envy, jealousy, or anger towards them, you are literally pushing the flow of affluence away from you. To experience affluence in this three dimensional world you must first experience it in your inner world. It doesn't matter how much you are visualizing being wealthy, if you're feeling negative towards those who are wealthy you are simply telling the universal creative force that you don't want wealth yourself.

The same goes for the people you have to pay as well. If every time a bill comes in you are filled with dread and find yourself swearing at the company that sent it, you might want to look at what kind of resonance that's putting out there. I was saying earlier that one of our great joys is writing nice big cheques for people who work with us. Well, what I'm challenging you to do here is to think about paying your bills in the same way. When I was financially broke, I quickly came to realize that my financial situation was a reflection of the way I was feeling about money. Although I was convinced that I liked the stuff, I was doing things that involved transactions with money where I was putting out some nasty lack vibes. I decided that things had to change and for those things to change, I would have to change what I was doing.

I started out by asking myself what was the most financially challenging time of the month and, as you can probably guess, it was the end of the month. I asked myself to pay attention to what I was doing to make it such a challenging time. As you can imagine my ego-mind was not one bit keen on that idea. It's not my fault. I just don't have enough money to make it through. I can tell you that for a while that argument had legs until I found myself with considerably more money coming in each month, but just like clockwork, in the last week of the month, I would still become financially frantic.

I began changing some things, and if you think these might help you, I would highly encourage you to follow my lead. Of course I'm not going to come over to your house at 5 AM tomorrow and check on you. That's your job. What I will say is, "If you don't change something, don't expect anything to change."

Here are a couple of the things I did that made a big difference to me and just might make a difference to you.

This first one is not a subconscious tactic for creating affluence. It is a simple conscious one. I began following a financial rule that we've all heard and very few actually do. I stopped spending more than I earned! I know that once you get on the old credit train, it soon picks up speed and then it's hard to get off. Later, I'll talk about money myths but for now, I just want you to know that if you think that the wealthy don't pay attention to what they spend, then you have never been around the truly wealthy. Spend less than you earn.

This next one is a conscious tactic for creating affluence that seeps into to your subconscious and starts that flow of affluence in a way you may never have suspected. When the bills would come in, out of fear I'd often not even open them until I thought I might have the money to pay them. This was not a very smart strategy as I never seemed to have enough to pay them. I began opening the bills as soon as I received them and created two files, one for "paid" one for "to be paid." Then I would open up all the bills and sit down with my cheque book and write the cheques for each and every bill that had to be paid.

Please note, I did this whether I had the money in the bank or not, because at that point I wasn't sending the cheque off. I was writing the cheque with the purpose of holding my intention to pay it. Right off the bat, this created a shift. I was now consciously aware of the bills, so going out and spending money I didn't have was no longer an option. *Simple, but profound!*

The next tactic was all about getting a state of affluence into my subconscious. I did something for the express purpose of putting me into a mindset of abundance. On each of the cheques I wrote the initials "G.B.A.M." G.B.A.M stands for **G**od **B**less **A**nd **M**ultiply. This gave me an inner sense that there was more both coming to me and to whomever I was writing the cheque. I also did something else, but you can't tell anyone because it is illegal. In tiny writing I would put those same initials on all the paper money I would get in my possession.

Right there you have three very simple, powerful affluence tactics you can use to begin shifting yourself away from lack thinking and towards more abundance flowing into your life. Now you can read over them and think, "Oh, that's interesting, maybe I should do that, and then do nothing which will of course bring you the grand result of no change." Or you can towel off from your swim in that river in Egypt called "De-Nile" and start applying what I'm sharing with you. That way you could write to me and tell me all your amazing successes and maybe, just maybe, you'd end up in one of my books as a success story. But no, you don't want that do you? No, I'm sure you'd much rather just keep complaining instead of actually experiencing wealth and abundance as a way of life.

Forgive me, I am, of course, saying all that with a tongue wedged in my cheek. I want to make you smile and realize how easy it is to let the ego-mind take over and dismiss what can make a major difference in your life. Remember that you want to make this make senses! I know you wouldn't even be reading this book if you weren't super keen on changing your financial situation. My making fun is just to point out that even the great secret of life is worth nothing if you don't apply it.

So, right now, think about how you can apply these three techniques. Also, think about with who you need to share what you've just learned and then get out there and share it with them. Every time you share this information, it will sink a little deeper into your psyche, and it will become more real for you.

Aside from not understanding that abundance surrounds us, one of the greatest challenges people face regarding money is thinking that their value is a reflection of their bank account. This is completely crazy, because your real value is untouchable by anything outside of yourself.

Your value is not changed by them (whoever "they" are) or whatever they told you. The only thing that changes your value is your own perception of that value. I truly would like you to go back and read that sentence over again, highlight it, underline it. Please do whatever it takes to make sure that it gets into the deepest part of your being. In other words, how you direct your thoughts and feelings about your value are the only things that change your value.

Like I said; understanding where your beliefs about finances come from allows you to choose to let go of any anxiety and frustration you may have been carrying around about money. The reason I say this is because the beliefs you have about money and wealth become your relationship with it. For some people this is a dysfunctional and even an abusive relationship that has more to do with control or the fear of loss of control than to do with having enough or not.

Does that make senses? Yes, I know I said "senses" again, and I'll keep saying it so that you stop and begin to take in the information to create transformation. Always remember that information without application has no value. As I said before, when you really get something, it goes deeper than making logical or rational sense. When we really "get it," we feel it, and then something changes within us.

Check whether you are now having some sensation of shift: A sudden silence in what had been a busy head, the gut reaction that tells you, "You're on to something here." Make sure what you're reading is hitting home and if you didn't have some kind of a light bulb moment maybe it's worth going back and reading that last chapter again and looking for what your ego-mind may have dismissed. It will be exactly what you need in order to become truly affluent.

Chapter 3

I Love It. I Love It Not...
Your Relationship with Money

As I will keep saying throughout this book, no one determines your value but you, unless you give them the power to do so.

In order to really get in the flow of abundance and have people bang down your door to give you money, (even if it's your Internet door), you must build a loving, communicative relationship with money.

Let me give you a picture to work with: How many couples have you met, seem close and intimate on the surface, but then after you get to really know what's going on, you discover that they've got some major below-the-surface resentment going on? Have you noticed how many of these kinds of couples play the "come here/go away" game with each other? They behave like cats. They scream for love and affection and when they get it, they often will push away the very same person they wanted it from. "Come here; I want your love. Go away; I don't want your love or affection." Maybe, you've even been in one of those relationships? Not only is it extremely confusing—it's exhausting! Eventually, even the most desperate of us will just give up and walk away.

Some people have a similar relationship with money. I highly suggest that you take a look at your relationship with the green stuff. On the surface it may look like you have a real love for the it, but if your "love" is laid down in a bed of shame and blanketed in stinky guilt, there's a very good chance you are going to (at least unconsciously) be pushing away the very thing you claim you want, namely money. Needless to say, if this is the case, you'll need to examine that relationship and find a way to turn an unhealthy relationship into a healthy one. If you don't, it's as if you are some poverty bound, dressed-in-tatters, super hero who has a shield of protection warding you away from the very thing you desire. This shield ends up disempowering you at every turn by denying you access to not just money itself, but even to the resonant energy that causes money to be attracted to you.

If, and this is often the case, you have bad feelings about yourself, if in some way you are carrying some kind of shame that tells you that you don't deserve an abundant cash flow, then this shield is in place to protect the crappy ideas you have taken on. In so doing you sustain the negatives that you feel about yourself. In essence, if you don't love, like, or respect yourself, it's going to be very difficult for anyone else to see your value and grant you your financial worth. Makes sense, right? Carrying around all that guilt, shame and resentment is like carrying an anti-affluence shield, so take my advice and dump it like a bad enchilada.

Here's something else to keep in mind: If you don't feel worthy, if you are carrying shame that was put on you, or you put on yourself, there's a good chance that you are resonating at a level of being worthless. Whatever you end up doing for income will likely be a way for you to give of yourself too cheaply. This, of course, is another power qualifier for your lack of value allowing your ego-mind to be right, by telling you that you're a victim, and it's not your fault. I've only got one word for that...

Bull!

You are not a victim, unless you decide that's what you are, and even then, you are only a victim of deciding that's what you are. Deal with the guilt, shame, and crappy self-worth. Start by making the decision to forgive yourself, and while you're at it consider all the other people you need to forgive because that's not adding anything good to your resonance field either.

Very Important Point I need to make something crystal clear. Do not believe all the crap you've been fed about forgiving everyone, that "forgiveness is a holy path." Here's why. Most of the people I've met who are preaching this kind of fertilizer are by and large emotionally shut down, full of buried resentment, topped off with a plastic smile. That, my friends, is not, never will be, forgiveness. Healthy forgiveness has a very important level of accountability. In order to truly forgive we must first take full accountability for our part in whatever it was (which doesn't mean finding a new reason to beat the crap out of yourself) as well as seeing "their" part in it.

Bottom line: Failure to forgive doesn't help you or anyone else, but know this too, healthy forgiveness has nothing to do with forgetting. In truth:

> *There is no real forgiveness of another*
> *until we learn to forgive ourselves.*
>
> ~*Dõv Baron*

It's perfectly reasonable for you to ask for money in exchange for your energy and your time. In a material world it's one of the ways you approve of yourself. Those who are holding onto low self-worth give away their authenticity in hopes of gaining approval. Don't do it! The price is way too high!

Look, I know that even at this early start of the book some of what you are reading might be a bit challenging to some of the stuff that has been plugged into your coconut for years and years. However, no matter how far outside your present belief system this is, always remember there is no shortage of money, so you are allowed to charge whatever you want for your services. Obviously, I'm not recommending that you go mad with this and start asking outrageous amounts because first of all you will have an internal ego rebellion on your hands. What you can do is start upping your fees in the kind of increments that both your ego-mind and those you are charging will be good with. (But again, be aware you will still piss off those who do not, and cannot recognize value.) So what I might suggest is that you could start at a 10 percent hike right away, then do something spectacular—put in 20 percent or 30 percent more energy and vitality. You will feel more valuable, and as a result, you will recognize the value you offer. Those purchasing what you offer will then see your value and over time you can give it another hike of 10 or 15 percent, and they'll happily pay it.

Remember: It's all about "value." The value you hold of yourself and the value you offer. Does that make senses? Yep, there's that word senses again. When you read about your value, how does that make you feel? What shift occurs inside that tells you that you are onto something, something important? It doesn't do you any good to just understand something intellectually. You have to "get it" on a much deeper level, an emotional level. If you haven't experienced the "light bulb moment" I talked about in the last chapter, stop right now, go back and reread these last couple of chapters. Let the ideas I'm talking about really sink in. When you "get it," when it starts to make "senses," come back. I'll be waiting for you!

Chapter 4

Be Grateful Later,
Stay Broke Now

It was almost a decade ago but I can still remember it because it was a wakeup call for me. On that particular day, my beloved wife was feeling a bit down and out of sorts. So while I was out at the store I saw the November copy of *Oprah Magazine* and I bought it for her thinking it might cheer her up a bit. Little did I know, as usual something way smarter than me was guiding my actions.

For three days in a row, I had been facing massive challenges. These challenges came in a wide variety, ranging from character attacks, professional attacks, to a personal journey back to my emotional childhood in which I questioned the very value of the love I offer. To say the least, it was a tough week! At one point I was in deep pain and although I knew it was emotional, my physical heart hurt. I gave my wife the magazine and went about my day. A little later that morning, I entered my office and saw that my beloved wife had taken a page out of the *Oprah* I had bought her and clipped it up on my computer. I would like to share with you what it said about gratitude.

"Gratitude comes easily when our lives are in order-when the bills are paid, the children are behaving, our health is good. But our challenges are what bring the chance for transformation. And it is for our deepest pain that we can be most grateful, because we know our hardship will deliver a lesson that refines our character. As you practice gratitude this month, give thanks not only for what you have but also for what you have escaped. When difficulties arise, ask yourself, "What is the lesson for me in this?" And when you can give thanks in the midst of your trial, know that are becoming your finest."

~OPRAH MAGAZINE, NOVEMBER 2000

As I sat at my desk, tears of gratitude poured down my face. I became instantly aware of all the things in my life that I had to be grateful for including the amazing woman I am blessed to call my wife. On the surface, it's easy for people to judge me as a tough guy. I lost my boyish looks during a rock-climbing incident in 1990 and my muscular body is evidence of my sport of bodybuilding. However, below the obvious, I am a deep thinker, a spiritually centered being, someone who likes a good laugh and despite the exterior, I am a big softy.

Gratitude Perpetuates Abundance.
When it comes to getting into that flow of affluence and attracting abundance into your life, at any moment you can tap into something that will generate and create the resonance, the attracting force that will bring you the abundance you desire. That something is **GRATITUDE.**

Truth be told, we all go through rough times when it's hard to find much to be grateful for. These can be the times when money is tight, health is challenged, and relationships with the people we love feel like just too much work.

Surprisingly, as tough as it can seem to do when you're feeling lower than a snake's belly, gratitude is the key to staying up in down times. In a time when the media are saying there's not enough to go around, you need to grateful for what you already have. Are you willing to accept the gifts that already surround you? Conversely, are you too busy focusing on what you don't have, looking for a catch, or telling yourself you aren't deserving? You can't see the abundance that surrounds you if you are operating out of cynicism or a feeling of unworthiness. It's like being red/green colorblind. The colors are always there, but you have no way of seeing them.

I know there are things in your life that you really want that you don't have. If that's where your focus lies, then progress will be slow at best. Gratitude is one of the greatest ways to get out of your own way. It's a wonderful way to realign your strength, power, and resonance. Gratitude not only perpetuates abundance and affluence, it perpetuates kindness, and respect. So dig in to discovering all there is in your life to be grateful for because as Cicero said:

> **Gratitude is not only the greatest of virtues,**
> **but the parent of all the others.**
>
> ~ *Cicero*

Let's face it. Many take the stance that they will be grateful when they have what they desire. To those folks I say there's a pretty good chance you'll never see it. You've got to be willing to open up and gratitude opens you to receiving. The more you sit around moaning and complaining, out in the world or even inside your own head, about what you don't have, the more you are out of sync with what you do want and in turn the more you push what you want away. The strange thing about this is that the more you complain, the more your ego-mind can justify complaining, because less and less abundance will show up. Your ego-mind will likely scream *it's unfair*, but nevertheless the fact is it's just your energy in motion, responding to your feelings.

What if, click, in the next moment you found the missing piece for you? Again, I challenge you to open up. The Universe is willing to supply you with exactly what you need. However, **it's difficult to get the ocean through a drinking straw.**

Write now, I mean right now, before you even go one step further, before you go to the next page, grab a pen. Write down five things you are grateful for, right in this moment. It doesn't matter if you do this in the margins of the book or in your journal, just do it and do it now.

Did you do it? No? Go back and do it. Come on, this is not going to help me however, there a bloody good chance it will help you.

Okay, done? Fab!

Let me ask you what do you think would happen if you repeated that exercise every night before you went to sleep? Do you think you would sleep better than when you go off to sleep worrying about all the things you don't have? Do you think you'd wake up in a better mood? You bet you would. What do you think would happen to your family if each night during dinner each person shared what they were grateful for? Can you now imagine the shift in your family dynamics for the better? Do you think you'd start appreciating each other at least a little more than you had before? Of course not all those things might happen but I'd bet many of them would.

So come on, step up and step into recognizing and expressing gratitude.

Why?

Because gratitude perpetuates abundance, that's why. And gratitude is one of the subconscious tactics of the truly affluent.

Just stop for a moment and really consider what it would mean to the quality of your life if instead of all that pissing and moaning we can all slip into, you became dynamically focused on gratitude. Hey, even if you didn't get one extra penny flowing into your life you'd be one heck of a lot easier to be around. So, make the shift. I know it's a cliché but, "Get an attitude of gratitude!"

This particular tactic for creating affluence hinges on the fact that even though you have goals and dreams that reach out into the future, it's all about staying in the present when it comes to gratitude.

Does that make *senses*?

Yes? Great! So before you read another word, stop, and take an action…Call someone, write someone a card or an email, and let them know that you are grateful to them or for them. While you're at it, tell them that you're showing your gratitude in order to take in the information you are receiving in this book to create transformation in your life. Always remember that information without application has no value. As I said before, when you really get something, it goes deeper than just making logical or rational sense. When you really "get it," you feel it and something changes within you. Make sure what you're reading is hitting home. A great way of doing that is by thinking about with who you really need to share what you just learned. Now I know as you read that someone came to mind. Whoever it was, get out there and share with them. Teaching someone else what you just learned is a great way to integrate. Always remember that your ego-mind will invariably say *I'll do it later* as a way of keeping things the same. Don't let the ego-mind dismiss what you need in order to become one of the truly affluent.

Chapter 5

I Know Exactly What I Want...
Kind of

Don't freak out, you've not missed church. Nonetheless, I'd like to share with you a powerful Biblical quote that's a great illustration of what I'm talking about. "For to those who have, more will be given; and from those who have nothing, even what they have will be taken away." (Matthew 13:11–12)

How's that for a bum deal? Or is it?

Bottom line:
We cannot manifest specifics with a general request.

Stay with me here because once you have specifically outlined what it is that you want, then you can begin designing a plan to achieve it. In the words of one of my songs from the album ***Resonations*** (available on iTunes): "Get Clear."

Please pay attention here because I have a warning for you. The ego-mind may have some challenges with you actually achieving that outcome and it may try to sabotage you by whispering stuff in your ear that will take you off target. So to make sure you stay on target I implore you to keep a success journal and monitor your progress. DO NOT change what it is you are going for until you achieve it. That way you can acknowledge your success. I can't over stress the importance of this. If you keep changing your desired outcome, how will you ever know when you achieve it? Make senses?

To achieve truly living in and from a place of abundance, what you desire cannot remain something you'd merely like. How many times have you heard people watch someone do something say, "I'd really like to do that." Then that same person walks away and you know as well as I do that they will never do anything about what they say they'd "like to do."

To bring whatever it is that you want into your life, you must develop an insatiable hunger for it. That means, for a while, it's all that matters. You vigilantly watch the ego-mind; you refuse to be taken off track. You know your direction and you will allow nothing to move you from it. At that point, all obstacles are viewed as challenges to be overcome, with each one giving you a renewed sense of focus. You meet difficulties with the mindset that there's always a way to overcome them, and moreover, you are committed to finding it. You approach, go through, and attend to your outcome without the option of griping or complaining. You keep moving forward; you make it a "must" and as a result, it will happen. Guaranteed!

That being said, the obvious question is, "What do you want?"

I realize that you might want all kinds of things: Better health, weight loss, soul mate, a new career and, of course, more money. Therein lies the problem. We get washed away with so many desires that we start behaving like the kid locked outside the big window of a candy store...so many choices and absolutely no access. So for now, because this book is dedicated toward the financial end of things, let's focus there.

Financially what do you want? Be specific! If you say; "I want more money," you're in trouble because I can give you five cents and then you'll have received exactly what you asked for—more money. So, at the risk of appearing blunt, how much money do you want? An extra thousand? Ten thousand? One hundred thousand? A million? Ten million? How much? Now let me ask you, is that a lump sum? Is it a yearly income or a monthly cheque?

Do you see what I'm doing here?

I'm asking you to get specific.

Believe me, the universe is even pickier than I am about details. The universe will give you absolutely anything you ask for as long as you are specific. I like to say that the Universe doesn't give a cat's fur ball about what you ask for because it's not judging your request...you are! The Universe will give you anything, but you will have to be very specific about what you want.

There is, however, one proviso. The universe will grant you absolutely anything except for a "specific" other human being. The one exceptional gift of being who we are is that we, human beings, have free will. As such, it's not possible for us to exert our free will over the free will of another. Sorry, but your fantasy person is arriving in your life only if he or she chooses to show up. But with the exception of a "specific" other human being, you can ask the universe for absolutely anything you want. However, at the risk of nagging: Be very specific! Be very specific! Be very specific!

I know you think you've been specific before. However, as often as I can remember, when something has not manifested for me or anyone else, it has generally had a lot to do with a lack of specificity. Again you may be tempted to say those three most dangerous words "I know that," but as always, I want to ask you to challenge yourself to check in and really find out if you do in fact know it.

The proof of knowing is in the specific actions you take and the specific results you've received.

Another reason we fail to manifest something is maybe we are sending out mixed messages to both those around us and to the universe.

Mixed Messages:

> Helen had been coming to see me for a little while. She had been in a live-in relationship with her partner Michael for almost five years and it was clear to her that even though there was absolutely nothing wrong with him, he could never offer her what she wanted. I'd done my best to assist her in getting clear about what she wanted in the steps to what she knew was going to be a rather difficult break up. As a result of her clarity, Helen believed that she'd been very clear telling Michael that it was over. However, even though he had left the place they had shared, he was still phoning her. The calls had become more and more problematic as he had begun to phone her at home in the middle of the night as well as at her place of work.
>
> On this particular day, as I sat face to face with Helen, it was only a matter of minutes before the real issue

became crystal clear: Helen had been sending him mixed messages!

She was telling Michael it was over but when he was on the phone crying, telling her that he loved her and he would change, she'd feel bad and keep talking to him about how he was a good guy and she just needed some time.

I quickly pointed out that this is, without doubt, a mixed message. At first she couldn't see it, but after a few minutes of walking it through step-by-step, she got it and it shocked her. What came forward next was the key piece of why she was not getting what she wanted, which according to Helen *was for him to just get on with his life and find someone he could be genuinely happy with.*

I asked Helen, "If that's what you want, why are you still taking to him when he calls?" Her head dropped down in shame and she said, "I just don't want him to think I'm a bitch."

"Ah, there's your problem."

Her head shot up. "My problem is that I don't want him to think of me as a bitch? I don't get it."

I have worked one-on-one with clients from all kinds of backgrounds for many, many years. I've never advertised and I've always had a waiting list. I believe there are many reasons for that. First of all, I deeply care about my clients. In fact, I will not work with someone if I don't find some kind of a bond with them. And secondly, I don't want to waste their or my time. As a result, the soft compassionate side of me has an equally direct style. In that moment it was crystal clear that I needed to use the direct approach with Helen. I leaned forward in my seat, looked her straight in the eye and said, "Which do you want? Do you want Michael to get on with his life, or do you want him to think of you as a wonderful, bitchless woman, because right now you can't have both?"

Clearly Helen's breath had been taken away as she found it difficult to ask the next question which she reluctantly spitted out, "Why not?"

"Because you are being cruel. You are sending a mixed message of come-here-go-away."

"But, I don't want him to hate me." The tears were flowing faster over the edge of her eyes and down the side of her face into her mouth as she tasted her own salty regret.

I could feel myself soften and hear my voice become more gentle. "If you have ever cared for this man, then you must let go of what you no longer want in order to make room for what you do want. And that means that he may think you're a bitch for not picking up his calls. If you care about him, let him go! Every time he calls and you start chatting with him, he ends up back on the 'Helen hook' and he doesn't get the chance to do what you claim you want—to move on."

Let me remind you why I told you this story about Helen and her break up. If you aren't getting what you say you want, then take a look at the mixed messages you are sending to yourself, to those around you and to the Universe.

Mixed messages are at the root of all your self-sabotage. Your heart and soul have desires and that's one message, but never forget that your ego-mind has a set of desires all its own which can and often is the source of your mixed messages. The better you get at communicating exactly what you want, the quicker it will show up.

Making senses?

Yes? Great!

Now before you read on, stop, and take an action...Take out a pen and paper, or, as I said before, write right on these pages, but do it. Write down one and only one thing that you want. Be absolutely specific about it. Go into every possible detail about every possible aspect of it. Do not allow yourself to be vague in any way what so ever.

Once you've written down what you want, speak to someone you really trust, someone you truly believe will support you in reaching your goals and someone who is a truth teller for you. A truth teller is someone who won't sugar coat it. They'll tell you exactly what they think. Now tell that person exactly what it is you want and find out if it's as clear to them as you think it is to you. Like the song says; "Get Clear!"

Once you've gotten absolutely clear on one thing that you want, you can begin to design a process for getting it. All too often, the place people get off track with this process is that they pick something that involves getting too many other things in order before they can get what they want. Step it back, pick one thing, one step at a time!

When you have walked yourself through this process in a way that has got you really clear something will happen. As I keep saying, when you really get something, it goes deeper than making logical or rational sense. When you really "get it" you feel it; something changes within you. Again to make sure what you're receiving here is hitting home, share what you just learned with someone. It's doesn't matter who it is. It could be the first person who came to mind. Whoever it was, get out there and share. Teaching someone else is a great way to integrate. As you already know, the ego-mind will invariably be saying some version of, *I'll do it later* as a way of keeping things the same. Don't let it stand in your way of becoming truly affluent.

Stop procrastinating. Stop making excuses. Do the exercise. It is a great way to create transformation in your life. Always remember that information without application has no value.

Chapter 6

Both Fear and Clarity Have a Price

I've talked about the need to be specific and that life, or the universe, can only deliver what we are specific about. You remember that, right?

Here's the truth of it: If you were to randomly stop people in the street and ask them what they want, 99 percent of them wouldn't have a clue beyond some generality like, "I want more money, I want a better partner, or a better job." Why is that? Why with all the resources available to us today don't people know specifically what it is that they want? Well, what I'm about to share might surprise you. Just for the record, I don't believe that people don't know what they want. In my opinion, people do know what they want. However, they don't let themselves or anyone else know because they have some level of bad feelings about wanting it. I'll explain that a bit more later in the book.

Before we go any further, I would like for you to really take the time to ask yourself this somewhat awkward question: Am I really willing to step up and ask for what I want? I can hear you saying something that resembles, "That's easy. Of course I am." Your answer may be automatic, but really consider the question because it's a lot deeper than it might first appear, and it will lead to some things that you may never have thought about. For instance, can you live with some people not liking what you are doing? Can you live with some people not liking you because they either cannot understand or have no interest in understanding why you are doing what you are doing? Until you are willing to step up and face the possibility that "they" will judge you, (think you're a bitch, a selfish a-hole or something worse) or that what you want will be out of range. (I'll go into a lot more details about the fear of rejection and why it's so important for you to overcome it later in this book.)

I'd like to be a little gentler about this, but I'm going to take a guess that you probably need to hear this about as straight as it can be, or you likely wouldn't be reading this book at this point in your life. So, take a deep breath, because I'm about to deliver something you really need to hear if you want to truly experience living in the flow of affluence that has eluded you.

So, here you go....

You have got to stop doing things just because other people expect them of you. If you want something because of a "should" (for instance, someone else thinks you "should" do it), there is a very good chance that even if you do get "it," you will also get resentment, anger, and a deep sense of needing to rebel, all of which will create a resonance that will attract more and more of what you don't want.

To get to where you want to go in life and have what you want, your own heart must be in it. What this means is that you will need to set your own priorities and not let other people set them for you. You will need to decide to spend your time, talents, and resources with the people, activities, or things that are meaningful to you. In fact, and I know for some people at first glance this may seem a little harsh; however, in truth it's essential to you being in the flow of affluence. **I highly recommend that you stop donating your time, talents, and resources to people or situations that are not fully appreciative of them**. For that matter, stop giving of yourself, in any form, to anyone or anything that is not somehow adding to the value to your life, keeping it on track, or moving you towards what you want and/or who you want to be. Listen, if you are not quick to jump up and set your priorities, there will be no shortage of other people willing to do it for you.

I know you're familiar with the saying "Do what you love and the money will follow." Well, when it comes to setting your priorities, whether you're a brain surgeon, a dog walker, lawyer or a garbage collector, may I suggest that you make the commitment to be the best surgeon, dog walker, lawyer or garbage collector you can possibly be? Be the best at whatever it is you are presently doing. Give whatever you are doing your full love and enthusiasm because that's the energy that will make you successful in the long run. Enthusiastic, grateful people attract to themselves others who are enthusiastic and grateful. So yes, do what you love and the money will follow. However, in the meantime **love what you do and the energy will follow.**

As I trust you are beginning to understand, for me this book's about a lot more than giving you a massive quantity of powerful knowledge. It's about getting you to apply that knowledge to give you the shift you need to be in the flow of affluence. Therefore this next section is another interactive part of this book. Once again you could just read it, tell yourself that you'll come back to it, or you could stop kidding yourself, grab that journal again, and really integrate what you're learning here. First off, if you've been sitting reading this for more than twenty minutes I want you to just sit up straight and take in a couple of big deep breaths. This will oxygenate your brain and keep you focused.

Now here's what I want you to do next. In order to keep your level of enthusiastic focus at its peak, write in your journal about what you feel your ideal life looks like. Most people's initial response to this is, "I have no idea what that would look like." But you know what? Most people don't look any further ahead than their next holiday. Again you can skip right over this or you can do your research and you know what you will find? Not one single hugely successful individual who doesn't have at all times at the very least a five-year vision and most often a much longer one. Trust me, if you're reading this and you are, there is something within you that is hungry for the next level so get out your journal and start writing. Go on. I'll wait for you.

(We have a process for this in the workbook that comes with EFM Audio Technology. If you're interested, you can find out more about the process at http://www.EFMAudioTech.com)

Look, even if you don't know what your ideal life will look like, you can make it up. Ask yourself if you did know, what would your ideal life be like? Where would you want to live? Who would you want to live with, who would you like to spend your time with? What seminars and workshops would you attend? Who would you have as your mentor/s? What kind of things would you like to do? What shows would you like to see? What kind of foods would you eat? What kind of a home would you live in? What kinds of parties or activities would you like to experience? What kind of clothes would you wear? What make of car would you drive? What kind of shape would your body be in? How would you contributing? What specific people or place would you contribute to? What kind of person would you be? What would you be most focused on?

Concentrate on what it would all be like, and even if your ego-mind is going *this is all crap*...do it anyway and do it as if it was all taking place in the here and now. Do it with every sense you can muster. Do whatever you can to see it, hear it, smell it, taste it, and feel it. Get emotionally and completely connected to your ideal life and know that whatever you are doing with passion and enthusiasm is in some way taking you there.

There will be obstacles; take that as a given. What you need to do is find them before you trip over them. Use your experience. The reason most people don't learn from the past is they don't examine what didn't work and so they repeat the same cycle and don't even notice things are repeating until the experience is in its final spin. Let me give you an example of what I'm talking about.

> Aaron had been studying day trading for about a year and in that year he'd been "paper trading" for six months. (For those not familiar with the term, in paper trading, a person does everything as if they were actually trading in the market except they don't actually invest real money. They experience ups, downs, wins, losses. Everything is the same as day trading except no actual money is lost or won.) Aaron knew that it was time for him to take off the training wheels and put everything he had learned and practiced out into the real world with real money. He was a little nervous but mostly excited. He'd been a very attentive student and his mentor was impressed with the fact that his skill level was way beyond that of someone so new to this game.

> Finally the day arrived. It was still dark outside when Aaron awoke, excited and ready to go. His family

slept soundly as he got up, took a hot shower, made himself a cup of coffee, and got dressed. They were still sleeping when he sat down in front of his computer. *How could a day that started out with such promise go so far off track in a matter of a couple of hours* was all he could think when he looked back on the morning. You see, that first day of "real" trading was somewhat shocking. In the past Aaron had consistently been up at the end of his paper trading days. On paper it was not unusual for him to be up as much as three, four, even five thousand dollars in a day. However, those were the days when the actual money in his bank account wouldn't be affected by what he was doing in the trading world.

When I saw him later that first day of "real" trading, he was noticeably shaken. We talked for some time about what he was doing, the method of trading he was using and the mentor's model he was following. We were both stumped as to why it had all gone so wrong. A week went by before I saw him again and now his disappointment had developed into full-blown frustration. By the time another week had come around, he was in a full-on panic. His bank account, which had been pretty healthy just three weeks ago, had taken such a beating that it was face down on the canvas and the referee was about to call a knock out.

"I really thought I knew my stuff," he said through the gap between his hands as he spoke with his fingers still cupping his face, "But you know what?

Maybe it was luck, and maybe my luck has run out?"
I've known Aaron for many years and I knew for sure
that he was grasping at straws. He was smart enough
to know it wasn't luck, but at the same time he didn't
know what it was if it wasn't luck.

Desperate for answers we dug deeper. Because Aaron
was convinced he was doing everything just the way
he had before, I wanted to see if there was a difference that he wasn't seeing. So I asked him to walk
me through a trade he had done when he was paper
trading that had been a winner and then walk me
through a "real" trade that had ended up a loser. I listened very carefully as he slowly walked me through
the steps of each trade. It seemed that he was right;
he was apparently doing everything the same on
both trades.

I was as confused as he was so I asked him to close his
eyes in order to imagine running the winning trade.
I asked him to get centered before he started and
to tell me when he really felt like he was calm, centered, and ready to go. He sat for a moment or two,
with his back nice and flat, his chest open, breathing
calmly with a slight smile on his face before he said,
"I'm ready."

I began. "Aaron, before you start, can you just tell me
how you feel?"

His smile got a little bigger and he replied softly with
a single word, "Confident."

"Excellent. Okay Aaron, as if you are in a real time movie, I want you to, without saying anything, run the wining trade"

We sat silently for what must have been about four minutes. Finally his eyes opened and a big smile filled his face. "Wow, that was amazing!", he said smiling even bigger than before. He went on to tell me all the things he was doing and how he was following the "spot-loss" rules he'd been taught and how it was all just working perfectly. I asked him to stand up and stretch a little as I needed him to let that feeling of confidence go in order to discover if there was any difference when he was trading with money.

Once he sat back down, I again asked him to close his eyes in order to imagine running one of the more recent real money trades he had done. I asked him to get centered before he started and to tell me when he really felt like he was calm, centered, and ready to go. Once again, he took a moment or two, with his back and chest open. He was once again breathing calmly and again, that slight smile returned to his face, "I'm ready."

"Okay," I said, "again before you start, tell me how you feel?"

His smile was still there, and he even gave the same reply as he had before starting the winning trade movie. However, this time when he said, "Confident," it didn't sound quite so believable.

"Okay, Aaron, as if you are in a real time movie, I want you to, without saying anything, run one of the money trades you've been doing." Again we sat silently, although this time it was much sooner before his eyes opened and instead of a big smile filling his face, there was a look of shock.

"What is it? What did you get?" I asked.

Aaron looked back at me as if he'd just encountered the burning bush on Mount Sinai and said, "It's obvious now, while at the same time it's so subtle that I had missed it."

I was intrigued. "Go on, tell me..."

He let out a loud sigh, and went from being up straight in the chair to letting his body collapse backwards. "It's so freakin obvious. Like I said, I was doing everything the same on both trades. At least when it came to following each step of the system I was using."

"Okay, so if you were following the system exactly, why were you getting a different result?"

Aaron looked me dead in the eye and he reminded me of something I'd shared with him and will share with you a little later. Pulling himself back up in the seat, he leaned forward and said, "You taught me that Genius has speed."

"Go on, I'm listening."

He continued, "Well, I was following all the same steps, but it was like I was doing it in slow motion. As I watched the losing movie, I suddenly realized that my mind was racing with anxiety about the possibility of losing the money and at the same time that put my actions in slow mo. That meant that I was constantly second guessing every move I'd made, and even though I was making the right moves, I was making them a couple of seconds too late and in trading that couple of seconds can be the difference between a series of wins or, as it has been for me lately, financial devastation." We both knew he had hit the problem square on the head. Aaron would have likely continued to do what he was doing, even though it wasn't working if we hadn't have stopped and truly examined what he was doing that didn't work for him getting his desired result.

Aaron's story is similar to many peoples' even if they aren't day traders. When it comes to dealing with money, most people become uptight and fearful and, as I'm sure you know, you can't think clearly in that state. By the way, you may be wondering if Aaron was able to turn his trading around. Yes, he was and here's what it took: I shared with him the outrageous piece of history that I told you at the beginning of this book about banking history and the concept that money is nothing more than an idea. That lead me to ask him something that you will in all likelihood want to stop and really think about. I asked him what the meaning of the money he was using to paper trade was. He told me that it had no meaning; it was just for fun and it wasn't real. Then I asked him what the meaning of the money was now that he was no longer paper trading. He was very clear about the meaning of that money. He said that it was his family's well being, and that if he lost it, he could jeopardize his family's future.

I laughed and said, "Well, at least you're not putting a lot of pressure on yourself." He had to admit he could see the humor of it.

The fact is that if you are given a hundred dollar bill when you are financially struggling it has a very different meaning than when your bank account is doing well. Yet when you think about it, there's no difference in the money itself. It's still the same bill with the same important person's picture on it. It's no less or no more real in either of these situations other than the fact you make it feel more real when you add fear to the mix.

Here's something you will certainly want to consider before you start worshipping at the feet of fear:

> *The thing you fear most is most likely to manifest*
> *because you fear it the most.*
>
> ~*Dōv Baron*

It's all about what you're focused on and how much attention you are paying to whatever it is that you are focused on. Stay awake and success is guaranteed. However, fall asleep at the wheel and—well—you can guess the rest.

Tony Robbins says, and I agree "Success leaves clues." However, so does failure. If you were to follow all the success signs in the road there's a good chance that you would end up at a destination called success, right? Well similarly, if the road is full of signs saying "disaster ahead" and you ignored them, you couldn't expect to end up in "Successville," could you?

Ignoring the warning signs is nothing more than self-sabotage. What I mean is this: In the short term it will always be easier to ignore the signs; in the long term the price will keep going up. Now at this point, your ego-mind can mess with you if you let it—remember the ego-mind loves a spot of the old anal-ization. It will entrap you in a downward spiral of "why?" It will ask you, "Why have you been putting off doing what you need to do? Why don't you follow through?" And you know what? There is a time and a place for that sort of introspection, but now isn't the time or place. Why you haven't done something doesn't matter. What matters right now is that you take that first step and do it NOW.

So right here, before you skip ahead, tap into your resolve and decide one thing you are going to do within the next five minutes to begin moving you towards your ideal life. It doesn't have to be some massive action—just do something within the next five minutes. Make a call, send an email, get up and stretch, go for a walk, a run, start a budget, write out a to-do list. Just do something to start the ball rolling, something that can assist you in building momentum.

There's just one more thing I want to add here. If you really want to experience the full spectrum of abundance in your life, it's super important to get yourself around people who are going in the same direction as you. Be around people who can get where you're going and who understand why you are going there. In your enthusiasm you will want to share your vision. I understand that and I truly respect it. But be discerning, as you will discover not everyone you want to share your dream with will be thrilled for you. Share your dream with others, but avoid discussing it with the nay-sayers and focus on those people who can support you. The nay-sayers will suck the life out of your dreams and in all likelihood after being around them for just a short period of time, you too will find yourself drained and feeling like *what's the point?* The nay-sayers are a virus and you must keep your dreams quarantined when you're around them.

Making senses?

Yes? Great!

Now before you read on, stop, and take an action. If you haven't yet done the exercise I gave you a few pages back about designing your ideal life, do it right now. Take out a pen and your journal and begin writing. Honestly, once you get in the flow of this exercise you will be shocked and inspired about where it takes you. As with one of the earlier exercises, once you've written it down, speak to someone you really trust, someone you truly believe will support you in reaching your ideal desired life. Please don't read another word until you do this exercise.

Okay, I'll trust you've written down what your ideal life would be like. Now, in this chapter I've asked you some very important questions and I'm willing to trust that you took the time to truly contemplate your answers. If you did, something will happened, something that could be as subtle as you began to feel a little warmer or cooler. It could have been as profound as feeling like you were hit by a bolt of lightning. As I've said, when you really get something it goes deeper than it making logical or rational sense. When you really "get it," you feel it; something changes within you. Really be willing to step up and ask for what you want. Don't let the ego-mind dismiss what you need to believe, think, or do in order to become one of the truly affluent. Remember, to get where you want to go, you've got to decide that you can live with some people not liking you because they either cannot understand or have no interest in understanding why you are doing what you are doing.

Stop procrastinating. Stop making excuses. Do the exercises. They are a great way to create transformation in your life. Always remember that information without application has no value.

Listen my friend, because this is worth repeating—stop donating your time, talents, and resources to people or situations that are not fully appreciative of them. It's a crappy way to build a false self-esteem because it's based on what you're not getting in return.

Be brave. Think about the things others fear to think about. Who do you want to be? Not just wealthy or married, but what kind of person are you working on becoming? These are goals of the highest value because in the pursuit of them you will become wealthy, if that's what you want.

Last but not least, I want to remind you (forget being casual about this; it matters) to truly get very clear about the meaning of money to you. If it's not a meaning that empowers you, CHANGE IT!

Now how do you feel?

Okay, let's move on…

Chapter 7

How to Dramatically Reduce
Your Learning Curve

Learning comes in different forms and what's wonderful about that is you don't have to make all the mistakes yourself. When I was in my thirties, I had a friend who was exactly ten years younger than me. We hung out all the time and I shared my best insights with him. He loved that I had traveled to places he had never been and met the kind of people he could never really see himself being with. He also was by my side as I made some colossal mistakes. One day we were sitting having coffee and we were both making fun of my most recent disaster. He suddenly stopped and said something profound, something I'd never even considered to be a possibility. "You know what I've decided? I've decided that I'm going to learn from your mistakes, rather than waiting to learn from my own."

Anyone who knows me knows there are very few times when I'm lost for words. This however, was one of those times. To use an English colloquialism; I was gob smacked!

He understood the need to reduce the learning curve by seeing what I had done that worked—and what hadn't worked. Brilliant! So why not reduce your own learning curve? Learn from the experiences and mistakes of others. Instead of reinventing the wheel, just take what you can from their life experience and tweak the process to fit your own situation.

Let's take this a step further and use it to deal with something we've touched on several times already—fear! By now, you're probably already wondering how to deal with the whole fear and money thing. The truth is, we could look at a myriad of different kinds of fear around money, but whatever version of that fear comes up for you, it can all be pretty much summed up by saying when you are in fear, you're not in the present moment. Fear is the great immobilizer. If you let it, it will stop you in your tracks. It will steal the words from your mouth quicker than a starving pickpocket could remove your wallet in a busy market place. If you don't stop fear in its tracks, it will fill your brilliant mind with cotton candy and have you acting like the village idiot at a Mensa meeting.

When your fear is descending on you like a London fog, you can do something to stop it, but first and foremost, before we even go a single step further, I want you to understand something that may shock you: Most of your fear is an illusion!

Here, let me demonstrate. Right now. I mean RIGHT NOW! STOP! DO THIS!

Take a breath in and then let a big breath out, as if you were sighing. Take another long breath in through your nose and breathe out again as if it were a sigh. Done? No, don't skip over it. Go back and do this now. It is very simple, very quick and it is going to assist you in giving fear its marching orders.

Okay, I'm going to trust that you have acted on those simple instructions. So take another breath in, and as you breathe out this last breath, I want you to ask yourself one simple question: In this very moment, is there anything to fear?

When you ask yourself, "In 'this very moment' is there anything to fear?" You will very quickly see that 99.999999999999999 percent of the time there is absolutely nothing to fear. I know this can be a little world shattering for many people, but fear cannot survive in the present moment. Fear is the ego-mind's manufactured idea that is projected into the future based on a perception of the past. Fear disguises itself in many forms that allow us to tell ourselves that it's not actually fear that we are experiencing. There are the obvious forms like walking around with a non-specific sense of dread to the more subtle versions like feeling a general sense of worry or anxiety. Fear can show up as mild nervous tension and/or all the way up to completely debilitating phobias. This kind of fear has been psychologically conditioned into a person via any number of situations and circumstances, and it is always a fear of something that might happen (future tense), not of something that is happening right now (present tense).

So your next natural question might be, *"Then why am I so scared?"* The answer is that the ego-mind keeps you in one of two places and in so doing keeps you fearful. One I've already touched on here which I'll come back to, and the other you will see is just as ludicrous. Let me explain. The ego-mind says: *What if... and it all goes wrong... like it did when...?* At this point the ego-mind is referencing something in history. It doesn't even have to be your history and it doesn't even have to be real; remember it's a "perception" of the past. The ego-mind then projects that history into your future. Thus at that moment, you are no longer in the present moment, you are in a future that is based entirely on the past. Therefore, the best way to deal with fear is to recognize that in any given moment there is actually *nothing to fear.*

So what can you do? Now I know this is going to sound way too easy, but really, does everything have to be hard? The answer to dealing with fear is: Just Breathe! Scientific research shows us when we are fearful, we actually begin to hold our breath and when you aren't breathing that sends a fairly obvious signal to the brain to produce the chemicals that will have you feeling fear. What this all means is that it's "you" and not the situation itself that is scaring the crap out of you.

Listen, it took me way too long to truly get this, and truth be told, it could take you years too. Or, you could significantly reduce your learning curve by choosing to learn from my mistakes? It's your call!

Again, nice and simple: The fear is caused by being "here" while convincingly pretending to be "there." Fear does not exist in the present moment. Fully returning to the present moment will, in so many ways, cancel your fears just as surely as a light shone into the darkness cancels out that darkness as if it were never there.

Let me end with one of my favorite stories:

> Anxiety knocked loudly on the door. I calmly got up and opening the door and asked, "Can I help you?"
>
> Anxiety looked back at me with little beads of sweat beginning to burst out on his forehead and with a tightness in his voice he told me that he was here looking for his big brother Fear.
>
> I replied that I was sorry to tell him that Fear wasn't here right now.

Anxiety insisted that this was where Fear was supposed to be.

I said, "I know, but fear doesn't live here anymore. It used to, and I know it plans to do its best to move back in at sometime in the future, however, it's not here right now."

Making senses?

Breathe!

Can you feel that? You know if you just slowed down enough to do that simple breathing exercise, all this will begin to make senses because you would have experienced exactly what I've been saying all the way through. When you really get something, it goes deeper than it making logical or rational sense. When you really "get it" you feel it; something changes within you. And again, if you did that exercise, you got a firsthand experience that fear is an illusion that you can conquer in any given moment. So, as usual, I'm going to ask you to make sure what you're receiving here is hitting home by sharing what you just learned with someone. Remember, it's doesn't matter who it is, but you know someone sprung to mind, right? Then get out there and share it. Keep in mind the ego-mind isn't in any hurry to change so don't give in to any of its *I'll do it later* crap. Don't let the ego-mind dismiss what you need in order to become one of the truly affluent.

Chapter 8

Are Your Friends Keeping You Broke?

Just before we began talking about conquering fear, I was pointing out how important it is to put yourself around people who are going in the same direction as you are. In this chapter, I'm going to do my best to have you demonstrate to yourself that this is much more than a theory; it's something of immense importance to every aspect of your life. I can't stress this enough: In order to get to your dreams, you will need to be around people who can understand where you're going and, just as importantly, understand why you are going there. In your enthusiasm, you will likely want to share your vision and you may be tempted to share it with questionable people. Remember that you need to be discerning because not everyone you want to share your dream with will be thrilled for you. The fact is that certain people, as much as you may love them and want them to be happy for you, will be the same people who will suck the life out of your dreams and being around them even for just a short period of time will drain the power of your dreams, and in the process your own power too.

If this seems a little overly repetitive or dramatic, I apologize. However, I do not want you to underestimate both the power of sharing your dreams with people who can and will support them and the negative draining power of those who would kill your dreams. And I assure you that by the end of this chapter you will be able to see with your own eyes the significance of the subject.

Before I can get into that demonstration, I am going to touch on something that I will go into considerably more depth a few chapters from now, so you can get excited now because it will help you to understand the experiment that you will be part of shortly.

Only very recently has science delved into truly looking at the realm of thought. True, science had done its best to understand the brain, but the mind, which of course cannot be pinpointed in the brain, well that was considered the realm of the philosopher. However, over the last few decades science has begun to look into those less tangible areas and discovered some "mind boggling" research.

The first finding is that we cannot see a thought, only the electrical impulses and the brain wave patterns generated by those thoughts. In addition, we make sense of our entire physical reality by the virtue of the thoughts, emotions and feelings we have about that reality and none of those thoughts, emotions and feelings are physical.

What science is discovering is that our thoughts become an organized field of energy composed of completed patterns of vibrating or resonating energy. If the accompanying emotional energy is strong, then those fields become energized together and integrate.

So what does that mean to you? Put simply: When you put yourself around people who cannot support your dreams, it's not as if they are willfully using their power to send "negative" or disempowering energy that crushes your dreams, but that is what being around them does. What it simply comes down to is that there are fields of thought, (yours and theirs) and fields of emotions, again both yours and theirs. The emotional energy between the two fields, although it is in no way limited to two, becomes stronger and energizes together, then the **energy moves to the dominant frequency**. I know we're getting a bit heady but stay with me here and I promise it will all click in into place very soon.

We know scientifically that energy moves to the dominant frequency and so you say, "Then there's no problem because I am rock solid in my dream." That's great except for the one great big hole in that argument: What most people do not realize is that they are sharing their dreams with a person or people whose approval they want. Now, whether you consciously know it or not, right there in that desire for approval you experience depletion in your energy. Energy moves to the dominant frequency and in such a case the one whose approval you require is clearly the most powerful energy since, after all, you are feeding into it. Therefore, what was once your powerful sense of certainty is now nothing more than energetic food for someone else's pessimistic view of what is possible or impossible.

Let me explain a little more. Every one of us is generating something called a Quantum Resonant Field (QRF). All our thoughts, emotions, feelings, and beliefs are part of this QRF, and each of our QRFs is interacting with all the other QRFs we resonate into our lives.

I'm building up to a more detailed explanation of your QRF in a few chapters from now, but what you need to accept right now is that this is science. Get ready, you are about to discover exactly how the science of QRF is playing out in your life right now.

The Experiment:

Just for fun, let's do a simple experiment into the discovery of your QRF. Here's what we're going to do: Below I would like you to write out the names of the five people you spend the most amount of time with on a daily basis. (No children under working age please.)

Person #1:

Person #2:

Person #3:

Person #4:

Person #5:

Now I'm going to ask you to do something for which you may have to guess if you don't have the specifics. It won't matter. As long as you are totally honest you will get a clear insight from the experiment. Next to each of their names I would like you to put what you would estimate their annual income to be. So it might look like this:

Person #1: John $50,000

Person #2: Paul $70, 000

Person #3: Sue $100,000

Person #4: Betty $25, 000

Person #5: Fred $15,000

As you can see right next to the name you would put what you estimate they earn per annum. Now sum up all five incomes, so in this case we are adding $50,000 + $70, 000 + $100,000 + $25, 000 + $15,000 for a total of $260, 000.

Okay, have you got your totals? Now if this is one of those places in the book you are telling yourself that you will get back to and do later...STOP! You need to do this exercise right away in order for you to understand what I'm about to share. I promise it's a profound insight! All right, now I'll assume you have written down the names of the five people, you've written down their estimated incomes, and you've totalled them up.

Now to the next step. What I want you to do is divide that total by the total number of people, which is 5. So in our case $260, 000 divided by 5 gives an average of $52,000.

Now let's take this to the next level of understanding: I would like you to write down how much you earned last year...

At this point there's a very good chance that your mouth is open due to the fact that your jaw just dropped. What most people discover is that their income is within ten percent of the average of the five people with whom they spend the most amount of time. This, my friend, is resonance, an example of the way energy flows to the dominant frequency. It means that if you are sharing your hopes and dreams with a bunch of people, even if you love them, whose only dream is to have enough money to pay the rent at the end of the month, that is where your energy will end up flowing to because, again, energy moves to the dominant frequency.

For those of you who did the experiment and ended up being the exception to the rule, because you weren't within 10 percent of the average, let me explain what's going on.

If you found that your financial resonance (income) is way higher than those you surround yourself with, it's likely one of two things. You could be playing martyr, always sacrificing to help others, in which case watch out—your income won't be above the average for very long. Alternately, you may be getting some serious ego strokes from being the financial big dog. If you don't believe me give it time and watch your financial resonance start dropping to the average that you calculated.

However, if you found that you are way below the average of your financial five a couple of different things may be going. It could be that you are running some grand entitlement program that says by virtue of the fact that you are here on planet earth, you are entitled to have other people pick up your tab. Now I know you're not one of those people, are you? But I'll bet you've met one or two of them, right?

The nice alternative is that if you find you are way below the average of your financial five, you have already moved your financial resonance and your bank account just hasn't caught up yet. However, there is one little proviso; if you don't become active in keeping your own resonance at that higher level, their financial energy will eventually just squeeze you out and you'll find yourself back below them.

Is this making senses? Can you feel the vast implications of the company you keep and the resonance you spend your time in? Okay, you got it. Let's get back to the resonance of your financial five. It's at this point in a live event someone inevitably asks, "So does this mean that even though I love my financially broke friends or family, I can't hang out with them?" It a good and valid question, the answer is, "Yes, you can hang out with people who are not in the financial resonance of where you want to be." However, I would highly suggest that you take absolutely any and all conversations about or related to money completely off the table." Why?

Because their energy will eventually bring yours down to their level.

That being said, the more you put yourself around those who are resonating at the financial place you want to be, the quicker your own resonance will shift. This is both a conscious and unconscious tactic of the truly affluent. I truly anticipate that this experiment really assisted you to understand the profound importance of your physical, mental, emotional, and financial environments. That is why I keep saying get yourself into a community of like-minded people.

I respectfully suggest you take a look at:
http://www.ResonanceCity.com

It's a join by invitation only private community of like-minded individuals where you can communicate with people like you. However, because you have invested in yourself by purchasing this book, if you go to http://www.ResonanceCity.com and hit the "Join Now" button, I'll give you a one-month free guest membership.

Chapter 9

Modeling: Don't Ask Losers How to Be Winners

Alana's face was flushed as she shared her wonderful idea with great enthusiasm. It was going to create a massive difference in a lot of people's lives and in the process make her a wealthy woman. Every sentence out of her mouth birthed a new idea of where this could go. She was on fire. Yet, just one short week later the whole thing had gone flat.

"What happened? You were absolutely on fire and now you seem kind of down about the whole thing."

Alana looked back at me with eyes that somehow managed to combine both frustration and sadness as she said, "It was a stupid idea. It will never work." She sounded like a scolded child.

While being respectful of where a person is, I'm not about to take any invitations to pity parties. Compassionately, I asked, "Okay, at least tell me how do you know it won't work?"

Alana quickly shared that she had told her older sister, and her sister had told her she was absolutely crazy and wouldn't work. She went on to tell me the names of two other people she had told who had similar reactions. Clearly by now you know she had done what you now know not to do after reading some of the earlier chapters—she had shared her dream with the naysayers, those who, "in the name of love," tear down dreams rather than building them.

I asked Alana one simple question and it was the one question that would later get her right back on track, and in turn, it may put you back on the road to your dreams. "How many of the people you asked have done what you want to do, or anything that is closely similar?"

The answer as you can imagine was a big fat zero. "So how would they know if it will or won't work?"

Alana became a little perkier as she, without realizing it, began to defend the position of the naysayers, saying why they did know what they were talking about and how she was foolish.

Again I said, "Please, just answer the question. Have any of them done what you want to do?"

"No," she said sullenly.

"Okay then, you may at least want to find out if it can work by asking someone who has done something very similar."

To get to your dream, you will have to believe it is possible or at least be willing to believe it is possible. One of the ways to begin believing that you can reach your goal is find out how it is done from someone who has done it before.

The best way to do that is to find a mentor. A mentor will be able to offer the benefit of his/her experience, expertise, and knowledge, and will listen to you when you need the support the most. Having someone who's "been there and done that" is one of the best ways to get yourself on track with what you want to accomplish or become.

Use what they did as a model for what you can do. Like we talked about earlier, you can learn from someone else's experience. A word of caution here: Modeling the mentor does not mean you stop paying attention. It does not mean abdicating your personal power or responsibility. When you are modeling your mentor you are following in their footsteps, but this does not mean ignoring your own intuition.

Just to give you a head's up, if you're ignoring your intuition while following someone's model, that's a great recipe for playing the "blame game." How many times have you heard that someone followed an expert's advice and it didn't work? I usually have two questions to that. First, "Did you really follow it, or did you just mindlessly go through the process?" And second, "If you did follow the guidance to a 'T' what do you now need to adapt from their model to make it your own?" All that being said, know that along the way you will fall, you may even get your ass kicked, but that doesn't necessarily mean you should quit. Very often a failure is, to paraphrase Thomas Edison, "Another way to not do it."

Use the mentor's expert insights to assist you in designing a plan of action, for...

Without a plan there is no action;
only distraction.

~*Dōv Baron*

May I suggest that you take a moment and sincerely think about what I just said?

One of the reasons you will need a plan to follow is that there will always be people who don't believe in you, what you're doing or the way you are doing it. There will always be those who are pessimistic and sadly, many of them will try to pull you down to their level. I have two things to say to that;

    1) Expect it! It's just the way some people are

    2) Get away from the people who bring you down and get
        yourself around people who can support your dream.

My best advice is always for you to surround yourself with people who can support your dream rather than your current reality.

Do not expect those who have given up on,
quit, or abandoned their dreams,
to support you in yours.

~*Dōv Baron*

Do not allow those naysayers to influence you. Don't feel obligated to accept their thoughts, or follow their limited reality of what you can accomplish. I'll say it again: Get yourself around people who can and will support your dreams. It's easy to quit when you feel all alone in your quest so reach out and find others. Put an advertisement in your community paper, join a conscious community, do something. Please pay attention here: YOU ARE NOT ALONE!

Remember, I've already given you an invitation to be part of a conscious learning community of people who can support each other, http://www.ResonanceCity.com. Being around people who can support your dream is crucial. That's why I am so strongly suggesting that you get some consistent high quality coaching. This is vital! Simply being mentored by someone who has succeeded wildly in the area of your interest can make all the difference in the world.

Get out of your ego-minded crap about not asking for help! Find a mentor and get coaching!

Realize this: The most successful and affluent people read books, attend seminars, join mastermind groups and clubs. They find mentors, network, and even hire expensive personal coaches to make sure they succeed. The truly successful know many things that those who struggle do not know. One of the biggest distinctions is that the truly successful do not try to do it alone. They understand that winning is a team sport. Think about it. Tiger Woods plays a solo sport, and he has been at the top of his field for years. You know what? Tiger has a team of coaches. He doesn't try to win championships on his own.

No matter what you may think of his private life, professionally he has been at the top of his game for a very long time. In many ways Tiger is also a great example of how we need coaches for different areas in our lives. Clearly, Tiger's golf coaches are outstanding, but, and of course, I do not know them. Golf coaches are experts at golf, not marriage. Get yourself a mentor for the areas in which you want to go to higher levels.

A personal coach whom you can relate to and learn from is of extraordinary value to your growth and development. A good coach is someone who will leverage your ego and fluff your feathers when you're feeling down. However, a great coach will see in you what you cannot see in yourself and they will push you to become the greatness that lies within you. A great coach will hold you accountable to that unfulfilled greatness within you and it's likely at times you may hate your coach because s/he will push you to your ultimate capabilities.

Remember, your coach/mentor is there to guide you, to point out the signposts and as brilliant as your guide maybe it's still up to you to step up and take the necessary action. I was having an on-line conversation with my editor on this project, Woodeene Koenig-Bricker, about how some people give away their power to a would-be guru rather than understanding that the teacher/guru/mentor (or whatever title works for you) cannot do "it" for you. Woodeene put it rather brilliantly when she said, "Expecting a guru to get you to the end point of your particular journey is like expecting Google Maps™ to drive you to your destination. Both can point out a possible route, maybe even the best route, but ultimately you have to drive there yourself." Well said Woodeene!

Regardless of whom you choose to have in your life—a mentor, a personal coach, or a group of like-minded people—the bottom line is, GET HELP!

Remember that the ego-mind and many of those who claim to love you will tell you that you are crazy for pursuing your dream. They will tell you to be realistic, but in the words of not only a very fine actor but also a rather wise individual, Will Smith, "Being realistic is the most commonly traveled road to mediocrity!"

Now I've got to ask you, "Is this making senses? Are you feeling it?" If you are not, then go back a bit. There's no shame in rereading what you haven't fully grasped; actually there's no shame in going back and rereading what you really grasped, it just takes it deeper. Read and reread as much of this book as you need to until something within you shifts: You get it—because when you get it, it will become painful continuing to do what didn't work for one more minute.

Okay, let's say you've got a mentor and you are heading out towards your goal. Is that it?

Well, aside from those people out there who are less than optimistic about your or their own success, you will have to deal with the liar who lives inside your head. This is exactly what we are going to talk about in the next chapter.

Chapter 10

We Don't Value
What We Don't Understand

No, this chapter isn't about how the wealthy wake up every morning with the intention of spending the day telling lies. Actually, this chapter is about the unconscious lies you have likely been told and maybe even come to believe about being wealthy.

With regards to what it takes to attract vast amounts of wealth and success, I have some bad news for you: You've quite simply been lied to and you've been conned into believing lots of stuff that is nothing more than fertilizer (also known as horse manure). People have all kinds of ridiculous ideas about what it takes to achieve vast amounts of wealth and success and consistently those ideas are...wrong!

Now I think you would agree that unless you grew up in and around a wealthy family, you probably don't know what the wealthy know about money and success. How could you? It would be like growing up in a village in Mongolia and expecting yourself to know how to speak English. Just give yourself a moment to now think back to when you were a kid; let yourself remember what kinds of conversations were going on around the dinner table or whenever the family would sit and talk. If you grew up in working class or middle class home I can guarantee that your conversations about money would have been very different than those of the wealthy. However, if you would have grown up in a wealthy family, the knowledge and mental technology I'm about to share would have been "common knowledge" to you and everyone around you because it would have been a part of everyday conversation.

At this juncture, I want to point out exactly what "common knowledge" is because I think most people have a misconception of that too. It does not mean, as many assume, *"Everyone knows that."* Common Knowledge means knowledge that's either common to you, those in your environment, or both.

At this point, I have to say that I know where you're coming from. If you don't know me one of your first questions most likely was, *Who is Dōv Baron and why should I listen to him when he is talking about attracting wealth and keeping it?* And you know what, even at this point, that's still a fair question!

Let me be absolutely open with you about where I came from so that you know how I easily understand what it can be like to be struggling, not just for money, but for wealth in all areas of life.

I was born in an inner city ghetto in Northern England and grew up in poverty with very few positive role models. Instead of going down the path of most people from my hometown, I somehow chose to use the despair that surrounded me as a motivation. By the time I was twenty-one years of age I had followed through on a commitment I had made to myself in my early teens and I left that environment to go on a spiritual quest. My journey took me around the world. I met, studied, and lived with spiritual teachers from a variety of disciplines and philosophies. On top of that, I ran and owned businesses on three continents. All of which would have been seen as impossible to do if I'd have listened to those in my environment.

Even as a small boy, I was a bit of a bother to those around me as I would constantly ask, "Why?" You see I was fascinated with why things were the way they were. Psychologically, asking "why" is a natural part of our development. As a result, some kids take apart their toys, old watches and many things that their parents would prefer they left alone. Still other kids ask that question and they quickly get shut down with messages like, *"Because I said so, that's why."* I was never particularly mechanically minded, so I mostly left those kinds of things alone. The "why" for me was about people, behaviors and the deeper philosophical why's. For instance if there's a God, why do children starve and is one religion right and others wrong. One thing that became particularly fascinating to me was watching so many people do the same crap over and over again, things that brought them all kinds of pain and misery. I wanted to really understand why they would do something that I, even as a child, could predict would have a negative outcome.

With a powerful set of "why's" directing my thoughts, there was one area that I couldn't ignore. However, it was an area that was somehow scary to look at, mostly because it would challenge not only what I had been conditioned to believe but it also meant I would be asking. It was a question where I somehow knew I wouldn't like the answer. You see I grew up in a home where we spoke about all kinds of things that most families would have avoided. We spoke of football (soccer), politics, and religion, three of the biggest no-no subjects. However, beyond complaining about it, we never spoke of money or the real reasons our family was poor. Then one day something happened that made a shift for me, at least in my consciousness about money. You've likely had an experience where you have held a certain reality, and because it's one of those all encompassing realities, you have no concept that any other reality could exist, and then...BAM! Someone or something hits you with a flash of insight you had never even considered possible and your whole world is shaken. That's what happened to me.

As I said, I grew up in circumstances that most people in a first world country would consider very poor. Everyone who surrounded us lived at about the same level of poverty. Our friends were poor, our relatives were poor and my schoolmates were equally poor. Then at age eleven my world got shifted on its axis. I was accepted into a new school, a school that was in a better part of town.

The first day in a new school can be an anxiety-producing experience for many kids. Everything is unfamiliar. New building, new classrooms, new teachers and of course, new kids. The first day of school arrived and I can still remember a slight sense of that nervousness. I entered the school wearing my new (well, second hand, but new to me) school uniform, which was something I'd not had before. The usual hustle and bustle of the first days of the school term were going on. As I looked around the school, a feeling washed over me that was, to say the least, unnerving. It was the feeling of being on another planet. You see, when I left for school that morning I walked, then took the bus and then continued to walk the remainder of the distance to school. You may have had something in your own life that when you focus on it, it's as if you are right back there.

When I stop for a moment and think about that first day, I am instantly transported back to entrance of the new school where I saw something I not only had never seen at school before, but also couldn't even imagine—beautiful cars pulling up; the doors of these cars opening and out came laughing children who even though they were wearing the same school uniform as I was somehow seemed different, brighter.

With second hand shoes on my feet and a leather brief case my grandmother had found at a rummage sale in my hand, I suddenly became dynamically aware that I was, as Oprah Winfrey puts it, "po." I guess the fact that we were poor had previously been an abstract concept, but now with a stark contrast looking back at me, "poor" was an absolute reality.

During those school years, I met many people who were affluent without doubt and meeting those people made certain things very clear to me. First, and very surprising, these kids were not necessarily happier than the poor kids. There were some kids I hung out with a little outside of school and even to me, a prepubescent boy, it was obvious that they weren't happier than the poor kids. They just had more "stuff." They were not necessarily more loved than us poor kids were. Even though "us poor kids" often came from much larger families with some major dysfunctions, there was clearly no shortage of family issues for the rich kids either. I knew this because over time, many of the kids around me who had problems would gravitate towards me for answers. (I can't imagine how I ended up going on to become a therapist!)

As I grew older (maybe inspired by those rich kids), one of the things I became fascinated with was success, and by that I mean success in the full spectrum. The things that make up the full spectrum of success for me include money as well as the lifestyle that offers. However, full spectrum success also includes health because, let's face it, if you've got a ton of money and you're too sick to enjoy it, you're not going to really be having the full experience of wealth, right? In addition, full spectrum wealth for me includes a spiritual connection and having high quality conscious relationships which includes other things that have very little to do with money.

Nonetheless, it was clear that these children of wealthy families had something I did not. I don't mean just having access to some level of their family's wealth. More importantly they had access to the inherent knowledge about wealth that comes from being in a wealthy family. These people had access to knowledge that I did not, and just as importantly, they had an understanding of that knowledge that at the time and for a long time to come, would have been beyond my understanding.

I hope you get what I meant there, because it points out something fascinating about human beings:

Human beings have no way of valuing what we don't understand.

However, once we understand what it was we were ignorant of…wow, whole new worlds can open up.

As I continued on my journey of life, I began meeting people who had an experience of life that was so far from the reality I had grown up in. I began meeting people who "understood" wealth in ways that it took me quite some time to truly grasp. I began discovering something that had been totally foreign to me—some people did not go through their lives concerned about putting food on the table, finding next month's rent or car payment, or wondering whether they could afford the new shoes their child needed. Now you may be reading this and thinking "that's nuts," and you may be thinking that from one of two places. It's nuts because you have never thought about life from the place of not having. Or, you may have thought what I said earlier was nuts because you cannot imagine that it is even possible to see life other than through the lens of imminent financial danger.

Putting myself around these people who truly understood wealth, I began to grasp that there was another way of understanding money.

It was a way that, in a direct sense, actually had nothing to do with how much money someone has in their account, while at the same time it was what indirectly put the abundance of cash where it was needed. It has to do with "money myths" and I'd like to share some of them with you.

Before we go any further, I need to ask you if this is making senses? Just think back over what you've read in this last chapter. What gave you a light bulb moment? What rang your bells, or sent shivers down your spine? Was there a moment when you "got it?" An instant when you read that most of the beliefs you have about money came from the conversations, or lack thereof, you heard around your family home? Was it the realization that wealthy children aren't necessarily happier than poor kids? Maybe it was opening up to the idea of wealth being much more than money and the idea that there is something called full spectrum wealth. Alternatively, maybe it was that quote **"Human beings have no way of valuing what we don't understand"** that shocked you to realize that it is possible to see money, wealth and affluence from a different place than you've seen it.

Whatever it was that created your light bulb moment, great! Take it in, write about it in your journal, and share it with a friend. Just let yourself feel it in whatever way works for you so that you can begin to now apply the subconscious tactics of the truly affluent.

Chapter 11

Money Myths

In the last chapter I told you that people who grow up or around other wealthy people have an understanding of wealth that can be completely foreign to someone who has never been in a place of abundant cash flow. What's intriguing is that for those who don't have it, money comes with a whole set of myths perpetuated by those who don't have it.

Let me explain. We take for granted many of the things that are part of our everyday lives. However, many of those things we now take for granted are the same things people thought of as "evil" before they were understood. For instance, at one point in history, even speaking about the idea that planet earth was not the center of the Universe or that the earth orbited around the sun got people imprisoned or even killed by those who believed such talk was evil. By human nature, we tend to be suspicious of what we don't understand. In truth, it's pretty much the same with money and wealth. If you don't understand it, you are likely to be suspicious of it. Did you get that, because it was short but also very important? Okay, I'll say it again a little differently. We have a tendency to mistrust, or not believe, what we have not yet developed the capacity to understand.

91

Consider this fact: Money myths are created around money and wealth by those who do not understand it or are suspicious of it.

Now I'm not saying you personally have been running all these money myths. However, there's a good chance some of them have seeped into your consciousness at one time or another. If you really want to get into the flow of affluence, it's going to be very important for you to pay attention to yourself as we take a look at this topic. Notice if you (or rather, your ego-mind) wants to automatically dismiss what's being said. Alternatively, maybe, you find that your mind starts wondering at a certain point in the material and the more you re-read it, the more it keeps happening. Maybe you suddenly start to sweat or get cold. All of these are clear indicators that you, my friend, have been running some major money myths, and your ego-mind isn't going to let go of them without at least a bit of a fight. Some of the more common money myths perpetuated by those who do not have wealth and or do not trust it are:

- If you go after money you might get it, you might not; basically it all depends on how "lucky" you are.

- In order to get the big money you will need to sacrifice your integrity.

- In order to get the big money you will need to sacrifice your family and friends.

- In order to get the big money you will need to sacrifice your personal values.

The fact is, and as hard as it might seem for some people to believe, it is absolutely possible to keep your integrity, your values, and anything else that you believe is an integral part of you while creating significant amounts of wealth. I know that's a pretty outrageous concept for those who are buying into the money myths, but then again, if you are one of the ones who is thinking it's an outrageous idea along the lines of having your cake and eating it too, then there's a good chance that at some point in time someone jammed some money myths into your head. Therefore, while it should be fairly obvious that when I say you can keep everything that is an integral part of you, let me be clear— that does not include any limiting ideas and myths you have about money. (One of the reasons you can't keep them is because they are not actually your own. I'll explain that a little deeper in the book.)

Now prepare to step back in amazement, I know you'll be shocked (but not all of you), but one of the most profusely perpetuated money myths is that "money is the root of all evil." The real quote is "The **love** of money is the root of all evil." Big difference! Now aside from being an incomplete misquote, this myth massively distracts from all the good we can do with more money. I mean just think about it…do you want to be evil? Of course not, right? Well if you buy into the "money and evil" connection, then aren't you evil by association?

This kind of crap is insidious. It directly and subtly makes its way into our psyches and blocks us before we can even get started. The fact is that there have been those who have used money in less than productive ways. However, those people are a minority. The truth is that when we become centered in the consciousness of money, we can use that money to alleviate some of what we see as injustice or evil being carried out in this world.

The bottom line is that when you are in the flow of abundance and money is flowing to you from expected and unexpected places all the time, you can choose if and how you want to have positive impact with that money. Take Katharine Drexel. She was the heir to a $20 million fortune at the turn of the last century. (That would be about $540 million in today's dollars.) Because of her religious convictions, she became a nun, but she didn't give up her money. Instead, she used it to found hospitals and schools all across America, including the first university for black Americans, Xavier University in New Orleans. After her death, she was made a saint by the Catholic Church. Even though she was wealthy, she clearly used her money in a positive and productive way. Her wealth, her affluence and consciousness, allowed her to use a fortune for good.

So now that you get the idea that money isn't bad in and of itself, what I'm about to share is likely to be unlike anything you've heard up until now, because what you've heard up until this point about wealth, you have likely learned from those who did not, do not, or are ever likely to have it.

Let me start by saying that those who grow up with and are part of wealth and wealth consciousness have no real grasp of poverty. Sure, they've seen the movies, they get the concept, but it's not truly real for them. By that I don't mean that they are unsympathetic or don't care about the poor. What I mean is they have very rarely had an experiential point of reference of poverty as being part of their personal reality because they have never lived it firsthand. What that means is that there is an ingrained, deeply embedded, unconscious knowing that they are part of an abundant, affluent flow. They understand something profoundly different than those who struggle, and it is this:

Those who struggle to make a living work for money, while those who live in the flow have their money work for them and this in turn allows them to work for something other than money.

You can imagine that if you grew up knowing you were part of an abundant flow, that belief would make its way into every cell and every fiber of your being in such a way that it would go beyond being second nature; it would be your first nature. In other words, you wouldn't have to think about it; it would just be the way that you operate. This understanding would change your entire relationship, not just to money, but to having it, keeping it and growing it.

Now you may want to go back and read that last quote again because it's one of those ones you will likely want to meditate and ruminate on. Having reread it and really taking it in, it becomes obvious that what needs to begin to shift within you to attract wealth is for you to look at your presumptions around money/wealth. Right now ask yourself, "Do I presume wealth and abundance or poverty and struggle as my default position when it comes to having an abundant flow?" Be honest with yourself. It's the only place you can begin.

I know it seems obvious now, but think about it, wealthy people presume wealth. What that means is despite the apparent circumstances, wealthy people look at their world as containing limitless opportunities for gathering wealth. This is one of the reasons people like Donald Trump cannot be broke for very long, and in fact, that is how the wealthy come back from bankruptcy and make far more than they ever did before. Is that making senses? They have a presupposition of wealth that allows them to see things like an economic downturn as having no permanent impact on their financial reality.

Now the question is, "Are there more opportunities for these wealthy people than there are for you?" You may automatically be saying, *"Well, of course, yes, they have way more opportunities."* Even so, stop for a moment and check to see if that's a fact or one of those presumptuous money myths. You see in my experience, and I have the research to back it up, if two people are presented with an opportunity and one has wealth consciousness while the other sees their world as one of lack, the one who is looking through "lack" lenses just cannot see the opportunities, even if they are sitting right in front of their nose.

I have a story to share with you that I think will really illustrate what we're talking about with regards to recognizing opportunities and staying in an abundant state. It's a great story and one of my best lessons with regards learning to be in the flow.

When I lived in Western Australia one of my mentors was an outrageous five-foot-four inches tall Scotsman by the name of William Todd. Willie was a well-traveled man who had served in the British army during World Wars II. He had signed up for service in order to avoid going to jail for petty crimes he had committed back in his hometown of Glasgow. To use Willie's words, there was "nothing spiritual" about him as a boy. He said that when his family would drag him to church on Sunday it was torture. You see he knew he was a bad kid. He was always in trouble for something so when he was in church and would hear the pastor say for committing his sins he could go to hell forever and a day, he became convinced that church wasn't for him. He said that he thought the forever was a bit much, but it was that extra day put him over the edge.

I've never served in a war and I do not pretend to know what that can do to a person, but I do know that with trauma we are always faced with either shutting down or breaking open. I think shutting down is always easier at first; however, coming out of that is very difficult and for many there is no way back. For those who do break open, their path usually becomes very difficult for a while, and there is often a sense of being completely alone. But once they become committed to the process, their lives invariably take a completely different tact.

This is where Willie found himself after the war. While many of his wartime buddies went home to find solace in the familiar and the bottle, Willie went traveling. I do not know all the details of exactly where he went or what he learned, but what I do know is that when I met him he was in his mid sixties and had been, of all things, an Orthodox Catholic bishop for many years. I spent many long hours taking in the wisdom that Bishop Todd would share. He became my teacher of "new thought" and Gnostic Christianity. At that time he had probably about 20 regular students however, maybe due to my deep spiritual hunger, we became close friends and he went from being Bishop Todd to just plain Willie. Even though the title changed, the respect I had for the man didn't.

> One sunny day, Willie and I were out walking together in the Hay Street mall, which is the main shopping street in Perth, Western Australia. This part of Hay Street has no traffic so as we stood there chatting, people would go by. Out of what seemed like nowhere a small child of about four or five years old came up to us. The little boy, who was totally cute, stood about three feet from Bishop Todd and said "Mister" a couple of times. We both stopped speaking and looked at the little fella. His hand stretched out towards Bishop Todd and in it was a five-cent coin. The little guy's eyes were sparkling in the way children of that age shine as they are filled with life. With a huge smile, he said, "This is for you."

> Bishop Todd bent down to the little boy's height, took the coin from his pudgy little hand and said with an equally big smile, "Thank you."

The little one giggled and ran off. Bishop Todd never missed a beat. Putting the coin in his pocket, he picked up our conversation exactly where he'd left off. I, on the other hand, was not quite as present in the moment. My mind was going a million miles an hour wondering how this enlightened man could take money from a small child. I was quietly outraged! Because I wanted to make it appear like things didn't bother me, I said nothing—for about three very long minutes. When I could no longer bear it, I interrupted my teacher saying in a very disapproving tone, "How could you do that? How could you take money from a small child?"

Bishop Todd smiled back at me like the cat who ate the canary. Clearly he was just waiting for me to say something. "What you saw never happened," he said mysteriously.

"What do you mean it never happened?" I almost shouted. "I saw that kid come up and give you money and YOU TOOK IT!" Any sense of carrying even a look of enlightenment was banished quicker than Superman's power when faced with Kryptonite. I was righteously pissed off and there was no hiding it.

Bishop Todd calmly said, "The part that never happened, that you made up is that I 'wrongly' took money from a child. What actually happened was I opened to the flow of abundance from the universe."

A little calmer I replied, "I see."

"Do you?" Clearly, Bishop Todd had his doubts.

He was getting on my nerves now and I was doing my best to return to an open place, even if I wasn't doing very well with it. "Yes, I do."

Bishop Todd inserted his hand into his trouser pocket and pulled out the offending five cents. He reached out his hand and offered it to me.

I think I actually moved a half step back as if it were contaminated. Bishop Todd gently said, "Until you can open to the flow of abundance you will always struggle with money." He was right and it took me way too long to get how right he was. As we continued walking that day Bishop Todd noticed beautiful birds flying by that I didn't even notice until he pointed them out. He watched couples laughing together while sharing ice cream and he also picked up at least three coins from the street that I just never saw. Bishop Todd was open to noticing the abundant universe that surrounds us all while I had blinders on, blinders that would all too often be the very thing that would stop me seeing opportunities and constantly creating too much month at the end of the money.

Does that last chapter make senses to you, do you get it? I mean really get it, not being like I was, and saying that you get it? Can you now feel the shift taking place in you, even if it's only for a moment? Even if it's at a somewhat unconscious level, right now at some level you are opening up to the affluent flow of abundance from wherever it chooses to come? Conversely, are you carrying around a whole bunch of restrictive rules that will inevitably stop you from living in the full spectrum of wealth?

When you get it, really get it, something shifts. Even if you've only got the very slightest sense of that affluent flow, when you sense it, go immediately into gratitude for it. Be present to it. The more you focus on the feelings of abundance when they show up, the more they will grow and the more you'll be in the flow.

Before we more on, I suggest that you take a leaf out of my friend Bishop "Willie" Todd's book and stay open to abundance flowing to you from both expected and unexpected places. How to do that is our next topic.

Chapter 12

How Pain Can Make You Rich

Think about this for a minute: If we are looking through a keyhole, we can never see the full view. When it comes to money, lack mentality is that keyhole! The vista is still full size; it doesn't change. It's your way of looking at the vista that makes all the difference. Just for a moment imagine what would happen if you could find the key, unlock that door, and then take another look? How amazing would that be? How much more of what was always there would you suddenly have access to?

What it comes down to is how much fear the individual is operating out of and how much potential risk they see in the situation at hand. Therefore, it is vitally important for you to recognize and access a couple of things in order to potentially shift your mindset. It's fear that narrows the view.

Is this making senses? So how can you begin opening up that view? First off, it is critically important to assess what it is that motivates you to get going toward the outcomes you are looking for. Let me explain: As you may be aware, some people out there, and you may be one of them, become deflated and awash with feelings of wanting to give up when someone tells you, "You can't." On the other hand, you may be the kind of person who, when someone says "You can't," becomes more focused, more determined, and more committed to doing "it" if only to prove them wrong. Let me say that neither one of these is right nor wrong; it's more about knowing how to use them as an internal motivation that possibly can crack through your fear and open up that view which will ultimately move you towards a place of affluence.

The major difference between the two is that the person who becomes more determined has, in all likelihood, made failing such a painful picture in their mind that nothing will stand in their way because they are just not willing to experience that pain. This person may start telling themselves, "I'll show them. I'll prove them wrong," and as a result they can become an unstoppable force. This is great, unless of course they are headed down a track that has no positive outcome, *(Don't marry that guy. There's something very creepy about him)*. When confronted, the kind of person we are talking about says, "Screw you" and ends up in a crappy marriage for twenty years just because "they" said it'll never work and this person is determined to prove "them" wrong. So, as you can see, these people can become very determined while they are also the same folks who can be very stubborn.

Obviously, quitting just because someone tells you "it" will never happen is a major downfall and crippler of dreams. However, there can be an upside. If the person you are discussing this with has the kind of authority, insight, and experience to guide you in such a way which spares you five years of struggle and a bankruptcy. Well, in that case "quitting" isn't really quitting, even though some would call it that. Simply put, it is paying attention.

You've got to know the difference between the two.

As I have spoken about in much of my other material, human beings are motivated by two primary forces—pain and pleasure. Now before you go off thinking this doesn't refer to you, please be aware this is a human condition, so if you've got skin and you're breathing you can be sure it includes you. As much as most of us would like to think we are motivated by pleasure, that is only the case for a few and even then, it's not necessarily the best form of internal motivation.

Let me share another story.

> When Mike spoke about all the great things he would be able to do when he reached his goal you could see the light in his eyes increase. His enthusiasm was contagious and anything seemed possible. I clearly remember that on one particular day, a day when around lunch, Mike had been spilling over with the wonderful possibilities before him. Later that same afternoon I found myself dragging this same guy out of an emotional pit of despair. Within a few hours he had gone from feeling like an unstoppable superman to feeling like the dirt under Superman's boots. What happened?

Let me explain. Imagine that you create a goal that you are working towards, and you're thinking about all the great things that are going to happen when you get there (you are being motivated by pleasure). Then on a particular day, you are feeling less than 100 percent positive or for whatever reason you just can't gain sight of your goal. Maybe something happened, maybe someone said something discouraging, or maybe on this particular day, your dream just seems too far away, too hard or just impossible for you. If you are motivated by pleasure alone, you're pretty much dead in the water because in that moment the pleasure just seems too out of reach.

That's what happened to Mike. Because he was motivated by pleasure, when the pleasure left, so did the motivation.

Now let's look at someone else, someone who is motivated by pain.

> Diane had known for years that she wanted out of her relationship. She had told me and just about everyone who would listen. One day her boyfriend Shane had been particularly mean and rude to her and from some-where deep inside she had found the strength to kick him out. It was painful to do because she did love him. Nonetheless, that smarter part of her knew that she had to walk away. Over the next four to five months she worked at getting her affairs in order and became in-creasingly happier and healthier. She had spent much of those first few months giving herself a hard time for staying with, as she put it, "that loser" for so long. However, the healthier she got, the more her ego-mind would "dry clean" the relationship she had with Shane. By the time six months had gone by, her ego-mind had cleaned, pressed, and hung Shane in his Sunday best right back inside her heart. Suddenly she was missing the guy she had less than a month before referred to as a loser. She was pining for the guy she had previously told me had treated her so poorly. Why is that?

Those who are motivated by pain will set a goal because it's just so painful to stay where they are. That's good. However, and here's where it gets a bit tricky, as soon as they are far enough from the thing/situation that was causing them pain, they will most likely just quit moving towards that goal and at the same time wonder where their motivation went. That is just what happened to Diane.

As you can see, both pleasure and pain can be great motivators. However, on their own they both have a very limited shelf life. So the natural question that follows is: What do you do? Well, I'll tell you, but you have to sit up straight again, take a nice long, deep breath in and out because this is important. The answer is simple: You learn to use both! You learn to let pleasure to pull you forward while pain pushes you onward.

Put simply:
Keep Your Eyes on the Goal and the Fire on Your Ass!

To stay on target with your goal it is of the utmost importance that you focus on both pain and the pleasure because that way you will never run out of steam. To say it again, in a perfect sequence you want pleasure to be pulling you forward towards your outcome, while at the same time using pain to push you forward even in the darkest times.

You may really want to understand how this works and how you can tap into both the forces of pleasure and pain beyond the scope of this book, if so, you can check out http://www.ResonatingRiches.com. In this six audio program you will be walked through the process that has driven many who had previously quit to keep going in the right direction no matter what comes up. If you prefer video, there is a very powerful version of this process on the DVD's featured in the Equation for Manifestation home study program which you can find at: http://www.equationformanifestation.com/order.htm

Okay, so now let's assume that you've got your pleasure and pain motivators sorted out, now let's move on in understanding how this works. If, for instance, someone has a goal to make a million dollars, and you've set that goal for achievement in say, two years and you are doing well, you're staying focused and doing what it takes to get there.

Now let's say it's four months in and you have already accumulated one hundred thousand dollars. You might be feeling pretty good about yourself. You may even feel like you deserve to reward yourself by spending a nice chunk of the money. Now let me be absolutely clear with you—I don't believe that accumulating money for the sake of itself is a particularly good or satisfying process. However, if you don't have your pleasure-pain ratio clearly set within you, there's a good chance that you will sabotage yourself from reaching your outcome by spending the money you have earned before you reach your goal.

This is where there must be a shift in your consciousness.

Of course, the next question is how to do that, and I'll tell you in the next chapter. However right now, just stop and check to see and feel how this is making senses to you.

Can you now let yourself feel that whether you are personally mo-tivated by pleasure or pain, neither of them alone will be enough to keep you going in the long haul. That's why it's worth repeating that you need to ***Keep Your Eyes on the Goal and the Fire on Your Ass***. So let's get into how to make that shift in consciousness that you need in order for you to become truly affluent.

Chapter 13

How To Win The Lottery
Without Going Bankrupt

Every millionaire ever born had one, every self-made millionaire has one. If you're not living a life of affluence right now, then sorry, you don't.

So what is it?

No, it's not a Mercedes, or a house with a pool, or anything of that kind; it's not even a rich daddy.

What they have that you don't but still need is: Wealth consciousness!

I know; wealth conscious, schmealth consciousness. You hear that kind of thing all the time these days. So what is wealth consciousness, or for that matter poverty consciousness? We'll get into that, nevertheless the astounding thing is, even though poverty and wealth consciousness are internal processes they can be experienced externally.

Listen I'm not kidding around here. "Wealth consciousness" and its nemesis "poverty consciousness" are very real, and they show up in obvious ways like the abundance or lack thereof your bank account and more subtle ways that I'll go into right now.

Make no mistake, without exception, every one of us can relate to the experience of meeting someone and getting a "good vibe" while someone else just "gives you the creeps." This is not limited to people; getting that vibe can happen in circumstances, too. You may have a firm knowing that when you enter a particular situation that "something's a bit off here." That inner knowing comes from certain places too. You walk in and the place gives you the creeps or conversely from the moment you walk in you feel completely comfortable. These feelings are caused by the *resonant field* of that person, place, situation, or thing. As I touched on a few chapters back, every situation, environment, and individual has something called a Quantum Resonant Field, (QRF).

Our Quantum Resonant Field broadcasts who we are at a core belief level. It's like a radio station playing a particular play list. Your QRF seeks to find a match for your resonance or the "vibe" you're sending out. This determines exactly what you can and cannot attract. For instance, if you're not resonating from a place of wealth consciousness, it is going to be virtually impossible for you to experience any long lasting wealth in your life.

Now before someone goes off the handle thinking this is some kind of new age mumbo jumbo, you should know "The Law of Resonance" is a quantum law. It's not something made up by some clown with his or her feet firmly planted in the clouds. It is science and you can look it up. There are articles related to the law of resonance in scientific journals that date back before the 1950s. Colloquial language acknowledging the power of energy has come a long way since the 1960s when we might have heard people talk about energy as vibes. People of that time used phrases like "I'm picking up the vibes" when referring to a person, place or situation. When we pick up the vibe, we do so in a way that transcends traditional concepts, and is best understood through the faculty of intuition. However, that does not mean that it's any less scientific.

Using contemporary language, we might say that a person has a "presence" or a place has "atmosphere." An event might be characterized as being "intense." These terms simply acknowledge that each person and situation has a perceivable energy, which is what I refer to as "resonance."

What is the Law of Resonance?

As I'm sure you would agree, the Universe functions according to scientific laws. We are all familiar with the Law of Gravity. It's what keeps all of us from being tossed off the earth into space. The Law of Resonance describes the way that everything in the universe is linked and communicating to act as a cohesive whole. And I do mean everything. Everything, including you, me, and what you want to attract—including feelings and emotions such as love—are all connected. The way that it all connects is through vibrations, or *resonance*.

I don't know if you saw James Cameron's multi award winning movie released at the end of 2009 called *Avatar*. This movie was very cool with absolutely amazing special effects. However, there was something at the core of the movie's brilliant screenplay that reflects what we are saying here about resonance. The inhabitants of the fictional planet of Pandora comprehend that there is a connection between all things on their planet and that all life is engaged in a symbiotic connection, which means that what we do to one thing affects all things. The native people, the Na'vi, not only comprehend this connection, but they are guided by it. They understand that everything in their environment is both in affect and effect with them. They deeply understand that what they are carrying around in their thoughts and feelings is impacting the collective life force of everything on their planet. So too, your resonance is both in affect and effect to your environment. We are not talking about environment in the way of recycling and using less fossil fuels. We are talking about environment in the sense of both your own outer and inner reality.

Is this starting to make senses? Here, let's put it into straightforward language: Things that resonate at the same frequency create resonance and resonance sets up the attracting force. This attracting force is also a repelling force as it determines what we either attract or repel based on what we are resonating.

Maybe you're into quantum physics and this really excites you or maybe the idea of reading anything with the word physics in it makes you want to take a nap. If you're one of the latter, stay with me. This is going to be really easy to understand and when you get it, it will blow your mind.

Quantum Physics explains that at its most basic level everything in the universe is vibrating energy. For our purposes, it is important for you to always be conscious of the fact that even your thoughts are vibrating. Everything about you has a vibration. Before I go any further, I should point out that to the quantum field, of which we are all part, there is no positive, negative, good, or bad energy. Those terms are our terms, the perception we put on the results we are experiencing. When you are resonating "positive energy"— such as love or gratitude —quantum bound subtle energy travels instantaneously out from you to the entire universe. The energy you have sent out then seeks its match out in the universe, and brings this matching vibration/resonance back to you. Here's what's so fascinating; the returned vibration/resonance has all of the same positive characteristics as the energy of love and gratitude you originally broadcasted.

This exchange of energy between you, the universe and everything in it occurs instantaneously on many different levels—emotional, physical, and even metaphysical. What's worth noting is the reverse is also true. "Negative" vibrations/resonance can just as easily be sent, and often are. This actually helps to explain why sometimes "bad days" never seem to end. What is happening is that you are vibrating/resonating "negative energy," thereby creating a negative resonance. The universe then keeps responding to your negative energy vibration by matching it for you, all day long! Why does it do that? Why would the universe send you a bunch of crappy energy back? The answer is simple: That's what you've been consciously or unconsciously broadcasting, and as I said, the universe doesn't see it as good or bad, it just keeps giving you more of whatever you are resonating. You could simply think of the universe as a mirror reflecting back whatever you put in front of it. It doesn't judge, it reflects!

To help visualize resonance, I'd like to share one of my favorite examples. Imagine that a student is instructed to hold a tuning fork by the stem while another student holds a similar tuning fork just a few feet away. The first student strikes his tuning fork, while the others in the class are instructed to simply pay attention to what happens. Within a few short moments, the un-struck tuning fork begins to vibrate/resonate. It comes into what is called *sympathetic resonance* with the struck tuning fork. Suddenly, the un-struck tuning fork is emitting the same note as the struck one. Isn't that cool? No effort needed. It just complies. **That's resonance!**

Again let me ask you, is this starting to make senses? Just stop for a moment, don't just rush through because this is important! Think about it. The second tuning fork didn't analyze whether it should or shouldn't resonate with the first tuning fork. It didn't judge it as a good or bad thing; it just responded to what it was receiving. The universe is no different! It merely responds to what you are sending.

Resonance exists all around you—not just in the science lab. No matter where you are, what you are thinking or what you are doing, you are resonating.

Think of yourself as a living tuning fork sending out vibes.

Before I go further, let me be clear about something. As I've already said and will keep saying, money is not wealth. Money can be a result of your efforts at work or even what some consider good fortune, but money in and of its self is not wealth. Wealth is generated by a state of abundance consciousness that you resonate out to the universe and, as a result, you experience abundance, in every part of your life. Wealth consciousness or for that matter poverty consciousness generates a resonance that is going to attract to you situations and circumstances that match the resonance of either your wealth or poverty consciousness at any given time.

Want proof? Here's a great insight into money and what happens when a person is coming at life from a position of "poverty" consciousness. Did you know that in excess of 95 percent of lottery winners eventually end up in a worse financial position than they were in before they won the money? A vast majority loses all their winnings within five years and nearly one third go bankrupt! Shocking isn't it? It sounds impossible. They get all that money and end up broke. You might even be saying to yourself that such a thing would never happen to you. Even so, let me assure you, if you don't have wealth consciousness before the money arrives, it will only be visiting with you for a limited amount of time before it takes up residence with those who have built the consciousness to house it.

You may not like what I'm saying, but I'm sorry to tell you that this is not an opinion; it's absolutely true. You see, when a person has *poverty consciousness,* a part of them will become uncomfortable with having wealth and, as a result, they subconsciously set themselves up to get rid of it. You can see that if you're looking forward to experiencing wealth in your life, and don't have wealth consciousness, it's going to be virtually impossible to not only get wealth but hold onto it. Napoleon Hill in his brilliant book, "Think and Grow Rich" said:

> *"There is a difference between wishing for a thing and being ready to receive it."*

That difference is wealth consciousness! Your wealth consciousness becomes the resonance you are putting out into the world.

Now again, you could just keep reading and absorbing all this insight. However, you do realize that this is powerful information, and you want to really take it in right? So, again allow yourself to stop for a moment and really let it sink in. Maybe take a couple of notes on what this has brought up for you. Think about what you just learned and with whom you can share it. Once more, I would guess that someone comes to mind right away, and that's good because sometimes we need to share something in order to really get it ourselves.

We are truly taking a look at wealth from the position of understanding that it all begins as a state of consciousness. However, you're probably wondering, "Where does poverty consciousness come from? Is poverty consciousness natural?"

I'll go into where it comes from in a little while, but first let me say that there is nothing natural about poverty consciousness. It is a result of a combination of beliefs, emotions, and thinking laid down over the years in the form of money myths. The challenge is that we so rarely stop and question these old beliefs, emotions, and thoughts. Yet so many of those old ideas were planted in your mind before you were even old enough to decide whether they would give you what you want, or whether they would be a massive obstacle on your path to abundance. If you want to know more about how and why we take on beliefs that just don't serve our greater good, and how to break them, I suggest that you take a look at one of my other books "Don't Read This...Your Ego Won't Like It!" Several chapters will really help you clear that up. The book is available on Amazon.com or if you want the full meal deal, in-depth experience take a look at http://www.QuantumMindMastery.com

Okay, you got a lot to chew on in this chapter, and there's a good chance some of what you deeply took in rattled your cage a little. That's great, because the moment you recognize that you are having some kind of reaction to the material, at some level it is shaking up the old beliefs, shifting your resonance and maybe, just maybe, even though there may be a part of you that wants to resist, it's starting to make senses. And that my friend is great!

Just one quick reminder before we go on. You are like that tuning fork and are resonating out from you whatever your wealth consciousness is, and it can only resonate with those things that have a frequency match with what you are consciously or unconsciously putting out there. Before you go any further stop, sit up straight take a breath and "feel" what that means to you. Let it make senses.

That being said, I'm going to stay with you now so that you begin embracing a deeper level of understanding about your beliefs concerning wealth consciousness. In order to do that, it's worth getting started by asking yourself, "What are beliefs?"

Chapter 14

Beliefs: How to Use Them to Predict the Future

Hey, just stop for a moment. Have you acknowledged and congratulated yourself? For what, you ask. Well, you are already in the process of doing something that few people will ever bother to do, and you need to recognize that. Take a look: One, you have recognized that something wasn't working in the way you were thinking, feeling about, dealing with or believing about money. How do I know? You're reading this book! Two, you're not only recognizing it, you took action because you bought this book. Three, you are about half way through the book and most people never even read past the first chapter of a new book (that's a statistical fact). Four, if you've been going through the exercises I've outlined for you, you are already shifting your wealth consciousness. Five, that means you are now shifting into the resonance of affluence. And six, you are already beginning to examine some of the limiting beliefs and myths you've been carrying around about money and wealth. That's why I asked if you had acknowledged and congratulated yourself. You cannot expect those who have not done the things I just pointed out to recognize the value of what you are doing here, so you must do it yourself. Congratulations!

If only for those reasons, right now, no excuses, do yourself a favor and stand up. Go over to a mirror, speak your name while looking in your own eyes and say out loud, "(Your name), you are now actively taking action to shift your consciousness and be in the flow of affluence." Don't wait around for someone else to do it for you. To get to where you want to go in life, you've got to do what you have not done before, even if you feel like a bit of a fool doing it. So, if you haven't done the exercise, come on, get up. The resistance is just your ego-mind wanting to hold on to some crappy old disempowering beliefs that no longer serves you. So go over to the mirror and just do it. If you want to you can even write to me and tell me how it feels. Because I'm telling you, you are doing what others are afraid of doing and that's why ten years from now, they'll be pretty much where they are, only ten years older, and you, my friend, will be in the flow of affluence and living your dream.

Talking of beliefs, which is the very subject of this chapter, why do you believe anything at all? Think about it. A question of this sort may seem to be, on the surface, a simple one to answer. But like so much of what goes on in the inner workings of our minds, a question like this invites us to explore a much more involved and often complex world, a world in which only real self-honesty and self-examination can lead to answers that have any real meaning.

Beliefs are the strange things that determine almost every aspect of our lives and yet by definition, a belief is something you hold to be true, but here's the shocker—if it's a belief then you do not *know* it is true. If it involved a principle or a law that you knew through empirical evidence to be true, you wouldn't need to call it a belief. It would be a "fact." Think about it—beliefs and belief systems are at the core of almost every organized religion and what are religions? They are commentaries of faith, which are not provable empirically.

Hence, religions require faith and belief, which is the acceptance of a non-provable argument as fact. On this level, belief and faith go hand in hand.

For many people, religion is not up for scrutiny because for them proof is not required for belief, so let's look at something else. Sometimes, when you are willing to question it, a belief can be proven false. When this happens, many things you held as a certainty can crumble. Often the beliefs that crumble are the walls that separate you from where you are and where you want to be. An example of this would be the belief that the earth is flat. No educated person living in today's world could consider this to be a fact, because no matter how much a person believed it, a flat earth is a physically false premise. Conversely, if you believe that planet earth is indeed round, science and empiricism affirm that this is true, and it is therefore no longer a belief, but a fact.

This is an opening for an even bigger conversation, the expanse of which is and of itself a book. However, to whet your appetite I will share one more idea:

> *Just because we do not yet have the apparatus*
> *to measure a thing does not mean it doesn't exist.*
>
> ~*Dōv Baron*

As you might guess you, me, all of us have a great many beliefs. Some of them are based on sound, logical suppositions and some will be based on something else all together. And some beliefs will fall dangerously in the middle—we haven't proven them to be fully true but we may not be willing to discover if they're false either. Often these are beliefs that are based on some historical perspective, and because of that are quite outdated. A good example might be the fact that the United States of America has never had a woman president. This is a very outdated belief.

Please understand that though our beliefs may be unproven or possibly downright lies, they do serve what the ego-mind perceives as an important purpose in our daily lives. They are the kind of beliefs the ego-mind just loves to hang on to because they become the automatic reaction by which we deal with day-to-day decisions that confront us. As long as we are on automatic, nothing much is going to change and that, my friend, is the way the ego likes it.

But you know what else? The reason so many people are satisfied with what they believe is because they are too lazy to think. I know it sounds crazy, but objectively thinking about examining our beliefs is just too much work for some people. Strangely enough, these are often the people who don't mind doing more than their fair share of complaining. Our beliefs determine the way in which we react to any given situation, because our beliefs by their very nature are based on history. What that means is most people are re-acting (doing what they always do) based on their history. Why should you care? Because, the ego-mind, which has been running your life, says that the future will be the same as the past, therefore there is nothing you can do right now to change things. The ego-mind likes things to stay the same because that makes them predictable. Therefore examining a belief or two is not an option as far as the ego-mind is concerned.

And you wonder why life can seem like a rerun? It's because even if the situation is or could be different, we just react in the same old way and turn it into exactly what we expect. Until we are willing to examine our beliefs, we remain victims of history and it's a history we are actively creating again and again. Here's a great warning about this from so many financial investment companies: ***Past performance is not a guarantee of future results.***

Just for the record, it's worth recognizing that beliefs may be instilled in us through many channels. Although there are many places from which we get our belief conditioning, the most common, as you can imagine, is from our parents. Now before anyone gets upset and starts thinking that it's *all* their parents fault, you might want to consider asking yourself, where did their beliefs come from? Probably their parents. Fascinating isn't it? You can now begin to see that beliefs become "false facts" because they have often been blindly passed down from generation to generation as if they were sacred truths. Wherever these multi-generational beliefs may have come from, you can be sure that many of them were imprinted on to our psyches before we were even out of diapers. Is this making senses? It's powerful, isn't it? When you stop now and think about it, it's some crazy logic. If we hold a belief as an absolute truth and we surround ourselves with those who hold the same or similar beliefs, we may see no reason to deviate from these beliefs—true or false—in some cases for our entire lives. The irony is that as much as we may want a better life for the generations that follow us, unless we stop to examine our beliefs, we are likely to pass these same multi-generational beliefs onto our own children and they onto theirs.

To say that we cannot know everything is an obvious fact of reality. However, to use that as an excuse to never truly look at our beliefs is a way to quite factually predict your future because when it all comes down to it, your beliefs are driving almost every area of your life.

Is this making senses? Yes, I know I once again said *senses*. Remember, I did promise that I'd ask that question so that you stop and begin to take in the information in order to create the internal transformation that has you applying the subconscious tactics of the truly affluent. You will always want to remember that information without application has no value. So as I've said before, when you really get something, it goes deeper than making logical or rational sense. When you really "get it," you feel it. Something has already changed within you and that will just keep getting more and more obvious. Once again, check whether you are now having some other sensation of a shift; maybe that sudden silence in what had been a busy head, the gut reaction that tells you, *"You're on to something here."* Make sure what you're reading is hitting home, and if you didn't have some kind of a "light bulb moment," maybe it's worth going back and reading this last chapter again and looking for what your ego-mind may have dismissed that is exactly what you need in order to become truly affluent.

I am aware that the material you are going through can be kind of shocking the first time you truly get it. So just sit with it, and write notes in the margins or in your journal. Think about who you need to share this new knowledge with and go out and share it. It will assist you in taking it deeper within your own subconscious.

There's one last thing before we go to the next very important chapter. I challenge you to really consider this: If you have been struggling to manifest a lifestyle of genuine abundance, at least for a moment, be willing to stop and question what it is that you have believed about money, wealth and the people who have it. You may discover that what you've been believing is nothing more than a multi-generational "money myth."

Chapter 15

Karma Down: Who's Been Sending You Crap?

I've talked about what your Quantum Resonance Field does a couple of chapters ago and in truth it's something I speak about in every area of my work because it's that important. If you find yourself on the edge of your chair with excitement at finally getting an answer to why the things that show up in your life do so, and at the same time wondering why this QRF thing keeps bringing you all kinds of stuff you don't want, I'd like to take a moment to go a little deeper into what your QRF is, because it is having a profound effect on whether or not you are getting the flow of abundance you are looking for.

If you know someone who drives you more than a little crazy because they are constantly sitting around asking you, and maybe even God, (insert whinny voice here), "*Why does this always happen to me?*", you are about to get the answer which is both simple yet profound: Your **Quantum Resonance Field**.

Your Quantum Resonance Field (or QRF), which is the science behind "karma," *determines all aspects of your life by allowing or restricting you to attract only people, situations, and things that are in phase (match) with your QRF. That's why this always happens to you!*

I'll give some of the easy to understand science behind that statement in a little while but for now let's talk about how I stepped through the door into my understanding of QRF.

As I mentioned, earlier in my life I traveled quite a bit and learned from teachers who came from a variety of philosophical backgrounds. Many of these teachers shared with me their profound understanding of the deeper spiritual questions that had been with me for as long as I could remember. My spiritual journey was both extraordinarily enlightening and at the same time frustrating. One of the reasons I found it frustrating was as much as I felt a deep sense of truth in all that I was learning, my anal-izing ego-mind was never satisfied because there was a lack of scientific data to back up what I felt to be true. Ultimately I was right back at belief and faith. This was very frustrating until the winter of 1984.

That winter I had flown with a friend of mine to Melbourne, Australia for a few days. For no obvious reason, I found myself wandering around a second hand bookstore while my buddy was looking at something in another store that I had no interest in. I wandered around, not looking for anything in particular, when I suddenly and for no apparent reason felt an inner urge to pick up a certain book. Opening it up and look-ing inside, I saw stuff that made absolutely no sense to me. Midway through every page or two would be some long equation that I did not understand. Based on my high school history with such subjects, I should have just thrown the book down and ran out of the store screaming, but I didn't. I read between the equations and although I cannot even for a moment claim to have understood a lot of what I was reading, what I did understand absolutely was in that moment, I had stepped through the doorway into a world that awakened an un-derstanding of the universe and how we are and it mesmerized me. It also ignited an intrinsic creative force within. This doorway lead me to

124

understand things about myself that I had never imagined and at the same time had given me a way to shut up that screaming ego-mind, because on the other side of that doorway was the world of quantum physics. The year 1984 was a long time before movies like "What the Bleep Do We Know?" and "The Secret" made quantum physics more of a general reference in everyday conversation. In fact, even for many of the scientists of the day, it was still considered pretty wacky. But it didn't matter to me; you see I had found the golden key to unlocking the secrets of my universe. I had found the third piece in a three-piece puzzle. I had the spiritual/metaphysical understanding; I was building the deep psychological understanding of the human condition and the missing piece, quantum physics, not only tied it all together, it made it all make senses.

You know what it's like when what you are holding in your hands is a revelation. It's like the words you're reading have somehow turned on a light switch you didn't even know existed. In this moment, you know you are already moving out of the darkness and into a new level of enlightenment. Through quantum understanding, everything I had learned from my spiritual/metaphysical teachers about how the universe worked suddenly had a scientific explanation. Now there was a way for me and others with over analyzing minds like mine to actually be able to embrace what may have previously seemed like ungrounded fluff. That also included something I had been having a great deal of challenge grasping—karma. I knew it happened, but I wanted to know how it happened. Most of the general understanding of what karma is appeared to me to be not much more than a celestial accountant who worked pretty much like Santa, calculating whether you've been good or bad and doling out good or rotten fortune accordingly. That didn't make a lot of sense to me particularly when I worked with one of my great teachers, Parthasarathy out of India, who explained to me that the word "karma" means nothing more than action. The real answer to why things, people, and situations show up in our lives is both simple and complex. Both classical and quantum physics discuss "the law of resonance" and when I buried myself in that law and the understanding that all energy has a resonant frequency and all resonant energy is attracted to energy within its own vibratory rate, I began to discover that we also are not only resonating energy, but so is everything about us, including our thoughts, beliefs, emotions and feelings. This is, in fact, one of the greatest oversights of the contemporary understanding of manifestation. Don't get me wrong, everyone who is on the law of attraction bandwagon is stating that everything is energy. However, very few understand that it is the combination of the resonance of the thoughts, emotions, feelings and beliefs that are actually determining what shows up in a person's life. These collective energies come together and create our personal quantum resonance field. We get back what we send out, so the bottom line is that each of our **QRFs is responsible for all those recurring patterns in our lives**. Our QRFs create our "karma." It's as simple as that.

Now do yourself a favor and just reread that last paragraph. Look, I know you read it, but did you get it? Honestly, it's worth slowing down for a moment to really take this in because it's life changing.

Okay, here's the deal. Unfortunately, many of the patterns that keep repeating are often negative or at least undesirable. What does that mean when you ask yourself, "What have I believed about people who have money?" What beliefs have you accepted about yourself and your earning ability just because someone else told you they were true?

These are of course just a couple of questions that can put you on the path to changing your QRF and therefore, changing what you attract into your life. Because your beliefs, whether they are "true" or not are having a mental and emotional affect on you and therefore your resonance.

I want to share with you what I discovered after years of research.

It's not nearly as important *how* you go about making money as it is what you *feel* about the wealth and money you make.

In other words, it's your beliefs about money that make all the difference. You may have heard things like that before, and maybe it just didn't make sense to your "logical" mind at the time. After all, we've all been told that *you have to work hard to make a lot of money*...right? Actually, that's wrong! In fact, depending on your attitude toward work and money, the harder you work, the worse off you can become!

So if you'd like to have what every millionaire ever born has, if you'd like to possess the exact thing every self-made millionaire in the world has, you'll need to resonate from a place of affluence at their level that generates wealth consciousness.

Remember there are no accidents in the quantum realm; there is only that which is in-phase or out of phase with your QRF.

Don't like what's showing up? Change your QRF.

Just check with yourself before you go on...is this making senses? Can you feel how with each chapter the knowledge is going deeper and deeper both in its content and within your subconscious? Great! Then let's keep this exciting journey moving forward.

Chapter 16

4 Steps to Freedom

Freedom is possibly the most driving of all human desires. Just stop for a moment and consider this because in one form or another I think you'll agree that we are all in our own way looking for higher and higher levels of freedom. That's a good thing because it is our nature to be free. But what is freedom? And how would you know if you actually got it? "That's easy," you say. "More money!" But is that it? Is more money really what freedom is? I doubt it.

Over the years, I have met and worked with people from all kinds of financial backgrounds. Some of the individuals who have hired me to take them from success to fulfillment and on to creating a legacy have more spending money a month than the average person has to keep a small family going for a year. In my travels, I've met people who are so financially poor that the poverty line would be a giant step up on the income ladder. In both extremes, I have met people who were free and those who were far from free. Money, I find, is rarely a guaranteed path to freedom.

I actually like the way I heard Oprah Winfrey say it best (and I'm paraphrasing): *Money just magnifies who and what you are.* She may not have been the one who originally said it, but the point is that if a person is emotionally constricted and repressed, more money simply magnifies that. Sure, that person will feel a little freer for a while, but it won't be long before that same person is talking about how the money has them feeling more constricted than they did before the money came along. Just read about any lottery winner. Most of them end up saying they wish they'd never won the lottery. I know, you're reading that and maybe thinking they must be crazy, but they're not. The money had just magnified whatever issues they had. So, clearly, in the long term money does not necessarily mean freedom. I could sit here and write another half dozen things that one might consider would result in freedom; things like more time, a different partner, or even a different government, but in truth freedom, just like success (or for that matter, failure), is an inside job. I really want to assist you in this so, let's get started on the inside job of reclaiming your authentic self to begin the process (and it is a process) of truly finding freedom.

One of the most important combinations to opening the lock that has kept you from truly experiencing freedom is in identifying what will come up in this next important point, so sit up straight in your chair, (honestly it will help), take a big breath in and read the next line which I've deliberately written in the first person: **What I don't look at controls me.**

Now, do yourself a favor, read it again, slowly, and really consider what that might mean in your life. Because the fact is, much of what keeps you from being "free" or experiencing "freedom" is the crap you refuse to look at—but that's over, right?

It is easy to tell yourself, "Ah, that's all in the past," but is it really? Think about it, is it possible that your history is having a direct affect on your finances? Well, whether we like it or not, it's true. What we don't look at controls us. Here's why: It becomes the undercurrent of our personality and determines how we see everything, including the lack or possibility of having tons of cashola. Just because "it" is in the past on a time line doesn't mean that you have actually let "it" go. Does that make senses? I'm sure you know someone who actually thinks they are over their ex and yet as the person looking in, you know with absolute certainty, they have not let that relationship go, even if it ended years ago.

Put simply, until you are willing to deal with your history, you will discover that:

Your past is leaking all over your present.

And stuff that leaks, tends to reek.

As you can probably tell by now I'm absolutely committed to making sure you get to a place of affluence in your life. That's why throughout the book there has been a ton of practical tools for you to apply. That being said, here's a powerful four-step process to get you going in cleaning up the history that is, in all likelihood, leaking into your present and has the potential of spoiling your future:

Step One: Watch for disproportionate responses:
Let me give you a great example. Who hasn't been cut off in traffic? We all have, right? However, what happens to you when you get cut off makes all the difference. Some people are just not bothered by it. They genuinely see it as "no big deal." Other people appear to not be bothered by such things, while underneath that glued on fake smile percolates a seething mass of rage. Still others have another approach altogether. Think about the last time someone cut you off in

traffic. If you noticed that you got way beyond mad and maybe even dipped your toe into the fires of pure outrage, that's called a "disproportionate response." (Even if this was all going on beneath the surface.)

A disproportionate response to what we are seeing (from the on-looker's position) is an incident that might have justified a 3 on the anger scale; however, the reaction was more like a 6 or higher. It's at that point you have the opportunity to look at this dispropor-tionate response and ask yourself, "What might I actually be mad about that has nothing to do with this situation?"

We all need to pay close attention to such a response when it hap-pens because it's full of clues. Any time that someone has a dispro-portionate response, it's a simple indicator that there is other stuff we are upset about. In that moment, being outraged at the other driver may seem like a reasonably safe place to express what we don't feel safe expressing in those other situations.

Getting to where you want to go is not, has never been, and never will be about waving a magic wand. Yes, I know that you would like that, we all would, but you know as well as I do, that's not what's going to happen. There will be obstacles, and as hard as it may be to face, you are likely the one who put them there, even if it was unconsciously. To become free you must overcome the ob-stacles that are set before you. Telling yourself and anyone else who will listen how tough it is does nothing but validate that it's okay to quit on yourself. A rich, fulfilling life cannot be attained by those who are willing to accept the mediocre. When you think about it, it makes perfect logical sense. Deal with your past directly or you will be dealing with it indirectly because it will just keep showing up over and over again in one form or another.

There Will Be Resistance.

Have you noticed that when you "get it," when you really know in one of those amazing moments you've come up with something that is pure genius, there's always someone who wants to tell you why it won't work? I suggest that you need to expect that there will be resistance. However, you don't need to become reactive to it. Sometimes the resistance is internal, (you scrapping with your own ego-mind) and sometimes the resistance is outside of yourself. Remember everyone is operating out of their own reality and it is the nature of human beings to want to keep those who are in their tribe, in their tribe. What that means is that members of a tribe tend to think and act within certain parameters because psychologically, they believe that these parameters will keep the tribe safe. If you've been part of someone's reality, meaning you were part of their tribe, (thinking and behaving within the parameters), and now you're doing something different, that can seem like a direct threat to them. As such, they may want to "bring you down to size," which actually means keeping you in their resonance field and therefore not challenging their reality. Are you getting this? Maybe you can even clearly remember a time where what I've just described happened to you.

Consider this significant fact: True Success belongs to those who are willing to do what others cannot do, or will not do. Let's face it; there will always be those who will tell you to take the path of least resistance. Let me translate what that means for most people: Don't make waves, go with the flow and "baa" a little on the way down that path worn smooth by all the other sheep. My intention is not to be mean; it is however to be direct in assisting you in waking up to the often painful fact that many of the people you have surrounded yourself with are not likely to offer long term support for your dreams if "they think" there will be some kind of cost or loss to them.

133

The path of least resistance
is filled with the corpses of the mediocre.

~*Dõv Baron*

What they don't tell you is...Those who do not have the courage to stand up for who they really are and what they really want die having lived lives that are, at best, half lived and all too often sadly forgotten. These are the forgotten lives of the mediocre. Those who fear offending others have allowed that fear to rule them like a fierce dictator who banishes freedom as if it was a plague. **You Do Not Want To Be That Person!**

I don't even for a moment believe that things will ever be what they were just a few years ago; wanting that doesn't even make sense to me. Everything has changed, including the economy and the way people look at and spend their money. I personally think that's a good thing. Many people's money mentality was based on greed and materialism. That's changed. "Getting all I can," can no longer be the way we view the acquisition of money and it may never be that way again. I know that can be a hard pill to swallow, but I think over time you'll realize that not only is that just the way it is, it's actually an improvement. What is important here to see is the huge gap between living in the mindset and experience of abundance, and operating out of greed. In fact, they are polar opposites. I know that for the onlooker who sees the result they seem the same, but in fact they couldn't more different.

Greed is just lack thinking turbo charged!

Before we get into that, did you ever see that great 1987 movie "Wall Street" starring Michael Douglas as the lead character Gordon Gecko with Charlie Sheen, Martin Sheen and Daryl Hannah as co-stars? It was brilliant and really spoke to the level of greed and mercenary behavior present in that time frame. The sad thing was that less than twenty years later we were breeding Gordon Gecko's like bunnies on a carrot farm. In my opinion, this insatiable materialism was at the root of creating the worldwide recession that began at the end of 2008. Although, I do not even for a moment think that getting a bigger car, house, diamonds or anything else is going to be the answer to your real problems, I do believe that we live in an abundant universe that is filled with everything we need and we are entitled to get our mental crap out of the way in order to experience more of the abundance that is our birthright.

All that being said, on your path to embrace and experience abundance, you must stay courageous in the face of rejection. As Thucydides said nearly 2500 years ago, "The secret of freedom is courage." Please remember, all courage is subjective. What that means is that what one person finds easy is not necessarily easy for another. So do what challenges you and keep on doing what challenges you and along the way give yourself the recognition for what you have already done so you keep moving forward. Are you with me here? It's not about comparison; it's about you dealing with whatever scares you. Every time you do, it is important that you stop and acknowledge your acts of courage because every act of courage is worthy of applause. At the same time, turn your back on complacency. Celebrating your success is an excellent thing to do and I highly recommend it. However, staying at the celebration as an excuse to not do "the next thing" is like still wearing your Christmas sweater in February. It gets a little stale.

Okay, so let's touch back on the whole disproportionate response thing that is Step One: There's a good chance that when you are having a disproportionate response it is because you took on someone else's reality and as a result abandoned yourself. So, forgive yourself, get up, and move on.

Now onto Step Two in our four-step process: Stop looking for people to complain to. Yes, it's hard sometimes...So what?

The truth hurts, but it always sets you free.

We have all heard the sayings "the truth hurts," and, at the same time, "the truth will set you free." What is it about the truth that makes it hurt? Maybe the real pain comes because the truth very often rises up into the mirror where we must see what we have refused to look at. Admitting (if only to ourselves) that we have been lying about what really matters to us at a deep heart and soul level is maybe one of the deepest pains of all. When we tell the truth, our "truth," we are forced to take accountability for our lives, and by virtue of that we cease to be victims of circumstance. What's wonderful about that is that we begin to own our power again.

At some level I know that you know that the freedom so many have been pursuing outside of themselves will remain elusive simply because it's not out there. However, it turns out that telling yourself the truth is the beginning of real freedom you can actually attain.

So, here's a simple and profound question to apply to yourself in your pursuit of freedom: **"What have I been lying to myself about, that it's now time to tell the truth about?"** Asking that can be tough, maybe even a little painful, but one thing's for sure: If you really listen to the answer, you are guaranteed to be on the path to your real freedom.

As I mentioned earlier in this book I grew up around a lot of poverty. In that kind of environment, I saw all kinds of people lying to themselves each and every day. I'm going to share some examples with you. However, please note these examples are not exclusive to those who live on or below the poverty line. Maybe, just maybe, you've used a couple of them yourself.

"He's not that bad. Sure he doesn't mind a drink, but not as much as…"

"My job is not that bad. Sure my boss speaks to me like a slave but the company takes care of my medical"

"I don't have that much debt. You should see how much 'X' owes."

"Yes, I'll change, but you know I could always win the lottery. I mean someone's got to."

"I'm not that overweight. I could knock off 20 pounds anytime I liked."

"Everyone knows it's family first so I don't mind putting my dreams on hold for a while."

"Okay, so I drink a little. I don't let it interfere with my obligations."

These are just some examples of the lies people tell themselves and in so doing abandon the part of themselves that wants and knows that they are capable of not only more, but also better. In order to do this you must move into Step Three…

Step Three: Stop wading in the river of Denial.

As much as the truth may hurt short term, the lies will hurt so much longer . Listen, it's your life, right? Then it's worth asking yourself, **"Whose rules have I been living by?"** If you were to really stop and question what it is that you believe and why you believe it, you might be very surprised to discover that much of what you believe is because someone taught you to believe it. Discovering that can be shockingly obvious!

As you probably remember, I was saying that much of what we have believed has been handed down like some ratty old rug we "lie" with from one generation to the next. So many of our beliefs are adopted and, like a baby left on the doorstep, we nurture them and tell ourselves that they are the fruits of our own deduction when, in truth, they are anything but our own. And all too often, these beliefs become "the devil spawn" torturing every aspect of our experience. People claim all kinds of beliefs as their own without ever even considering whether it is something they truly believe of their own volition or something that was given to them. Stop for a moment and really think about that...

If you didn't choose it, it's not really yours.

Did that hit home? *"If you didn't choose it, it's not really yours."*

If we simply accept beliefs without question, then we are living by other people's rules. We are looking at life through someone else's distorted lenses of reality. Asking those difficult questions, the ones you would much rather skip over, is a fantastic way to reclaim your power. Owning your power by clearing your history starts with asking yourself those difficult questions over and over again until you get to "your own truth," and maybe even crawl out of that river Denial. Be warned: These questions may shake the very foundations of what you believe, particularly about who you think you are. In a nutshell, if you really want to be free, you may want to keep in the front of your mind that you are not free because some part of you has a belief that keeps you from being free. Naturally that leads us into...

Step Four: Question your beliefs!

We've already talked about it, and we will again because it's so important. Every belief you hold, you have because you accepted it from somewhere, at some point in time. In all likelihood, you received and accepted that belief before you were even old enough to consider whether that belief would be of value to you, let alone resonate with the truth of who you are at a deeply authentic level.

Consequently, any belief that you have is worth examining because letting go of one restrictive belief can be like turning the key to open up what has been a mental prison cell. As difficult as it may seem, turning that key will let you step out onto the new ground that awaits you, a place like nothing you've experienced before. A place where you will be lighter and you will fly on the wings of possibility.

These 4 steps will immediately begin shifting your QRF to attract more situations that facilitate greater and greater levels of freedom, which of course includes more moolah, the green stuff, dough, or moneeeeeeeeeey.

All right, we are back at the consistent question…Is this making senses? This was a big chapter; there was a lot of meat in it, so take your time digesting it. Did you go through the four steps? Come on now, I know you don't want this book, or the knowledge and wisdom within these pages to end up being more "shelf help" (looks impressive on your bookshelf but did nothing with it). Did you really let it in? I mean did you really let yourself feel the truth of the fact that more money is only one small part of what it takes to be free? As much as we want financial freedom, the freedom we are looking for is from the restrictive beliefs we have, particularly around money and wealth. That's why in this chapter I've asked you to really consider if your past is really "done" or are you carrying around a bunch of emotional baggage that is creating all kinds of less than desirable disproportionate responses and results.

Again, think about who you need to share this with. Who was the first person that flashed in your mind that you know truly needs to get this? Go share it with them, so that you integrate this knowledge at a deeper and deeper level yourself. Also, keep in mind that they may not agree with you; they may even object. That's not the point! You now know to expect obstacles; they are a sign of progress.

That being said recognize this: Those who are outstandingly successful in life have the ability to see beyond what is perceived as reality. They choose to dream bigger than the reality they find themselves surrounded by. They are willing to believe with all their hearts, souls, and minds that "it" can be different than it has always been. The question is, "Are you willing?"

Chapter 17

The Power of Contribution in Making You Wealthy

Once you have applied the first four steps I gave you in the last chapter, certain things start to happen. First, your quantum resonance field begins to shift, and as a result, you begin to notice things, circumstances, and situations that you would have previously completely missed. If you think that's no big deal, think again. Initially it's important that you begin to notice "what's not working." This will, as I pointed out earlier, give you your pain motivation. It's worth noting that this pain will be very different than the pain you experienced when you previously were figuratively or literally stomping your feet in frustration that something just didn't work. No, with the shift in consciousness I am referring to, there is very often a calm cool awareness that what you have been doing has, in fact, been working at creating a certain result. However, in your newly awakened state you will come to realize that while it has been working, it hasn't been bringing you the results you are truly desirous of. At this point, your pain motivation very often becomes calm, cool, and collected with a single-minded certainty of what needs to change. It is from this point that the real shift begins. You begin to question what might work in bringing what it is that you really want and what you can do about it. Your consciousness now becomes focused on noticing what's working, and further possibilities of what may work.

It's at this point that you will notice an opening in your consciousness, an opening that had previously been filled with the ramblings of the ego-mind's repetitious limited beliefs. It's as if your mind which had been suffocating under the weight of mental confusion can now breathe freely again. As you begin to make the shift away from poverty consciousness and towards wealth consciousness, instead of being focused on how you don't want to be in the same financial straits you were in at some point in your history, you now become focused on experiences that created a feeling of wealth. You center your thinking around experiences that are deeply meaningful, not as some childish distain of those who have less than you, but rather as a way to make a contribution.

This is in fact part of the competitive edge you have been looking for. Although by now you are likely beginning to deeply realize that the competitive edge is not over anyone else, it's over the crappy limited thinking that's been blocking you from being in the flow of affluence.

Now to get back to contribution. When I say "contribution," please understand that this is not limited to being a monetary donation although that can be a part of it. A dear friend of mine, Teri Hawkins, is a Master Teacher, bestselling Author, minister, and someone who, like me, has a passion for changing the world. Teri knows what it's like to receive charity and also to give a helping hand. Teri recovered from "permanent" paralysis to become a world-class athlete. By the age of thirty, she had gone from a childhood of poverty to becoming a highly successful millionaire who has been honored many times for her philanthropy. Teri, her husband Steve and their team run a Not for Profit group called "Our Own 2 Hands." Teri and I were sitting around in my office one day having a conversation about the pros and cons of charity when Teri put it so well. "We are not a charity. Charities can, in some cases, become a crutch that keeps the receiver dependant. Our organization is all about assisting individuals develop what they need in order to become independent."

Teri's Not for Profit "Our Own 2 Hands" honors those who use their own two hands to make a difference in the world. Rather than giving to people in need, this nonprofit organization gives to those who inspire others. Co-founders Teri and Steve Hawkins are dedicated to changing the world's thinking about giving—one inspiration at a time. As a child of poverty, Teri is crystal clear on how damaging charity can be. She says, "Nothing damaged my sense of self-worth more than charity. Nothing built it up more than being given the opportunity to give. "Our Own 2 Hands" gives to the world's givers!"

Does that make senses? Are you really letting that soak in? All too often our giving, rather that empowering the receiver, disempowers them.

You know the old proverb: "Give a man a fish; you have fed him for today. Teach a man to fish; and you have fed him for a lifetime." Well there's an even better one that fits with what we are discussing with regards to contribution: "Give a man a fish; you have fed him for today. Teach a man to fish; you have fed him for a lifetime. Teach a man to sell fish and he eats steak." It's not mine, I actually don't know where it came from, but it definitely makes the point.

In the way I'm referring to it, "contribution" means being focused on the understanding that at every level your focus becomes about creating wealth, not only for you, but also for and with others.

Right now though, the only real question to ask yourself is how can I contribute more? I understand that at this point in your life you could be looking at a rather sad bank balance and again I caution you not to, not even for a single moment, consider that your bank balance is representative of your true worth. No matter what your bank balance says, you can always contribute.

In popular culture, a lot of thinking revolves around the idea of giving in order to receive. This concept is even being backed up with sayings that have soft Biblical references, for example, "Give and it shall be returned to you." (If I've heard people tell me this ten times, I've heard it a hundred times.) To me this kind of thinking sets up some bogus charitable gambling mentality along the lines of, "I put a twenty down on AIDS relief and now I'm waiting for it to flow back to me as two hundred." When our "gamble" doesn't appear to come back the way we expected, we begin to think maybe we didn't give enough or maybe we just stop giving because it "never" comes back. This is not at all what contribution is all about. I have said and will keep saying how important it is to give, but doing it as if you are dealing with a spiritual investment broker is a less than stellar approach. Now listen, I'm all for your getting back what you put in to something. I can even be very genuinely happy for you getting some interest on your investment. However, giving and contributing in the way we were just speaking about is all in relation to coming from a place of lack. When you give from a place of abundant flow, of being in the flow of affluence, that there is no lack, therefore you are not attached to a return, then you are in a place of contribution via affluence rather than lack, and strangely enough, that's when it comes back to you in spades.

I want to share another powerful subconscious technique with you that I used many years ago to begin moving myself away from lack thinking and into the space of being in the affluent flow. It's a superb technique and I still use it today. Now before I go on, I know that you know that everything I share with you, whether within the pages of this book or at any of my live events has to have a real world practicality or I'm just not going to put it out there. Well, this is more of a metaphysical technique, so if this kind of thing is a little unfamiliar to you, you may feel a little weird doing it. However, even though it's more abstract I want you to stop yourself from dismissing it, because once you get into it, I guarantee it's a lot of fun. It will definitely put a smile on your face, and it will have you feeling totally abundant even if your bank account disagrees.

To set the stage, I would like to invite you to come back in time with me to a place in my history, before I was teaching the kind of material you are enjoying here, the early years of my life when I was living in Australia. Let me begin by saying that when I lived in Australia, there was a time when I was going through a few financial challenges. My business partner and I had just started our business and we had sunk all our money into it. In the beginning there wasn't much coming back out. At that time I was deeply involved in studying metaphysical law and the whole idea that you and I live in an abundant universe. I was struggling with the understanding that being abundant didn't just mean that I was receiving a lot but that it meant that I needed to be open to abundance flowing through me, as well as to me. I was challenged to give in order to create the space for more to come in. As you can imagine, with any new business, there were lots of bills and not much income, so giving was not only something I was very challenged to do, but my ego-mind also had a whole truckload of reasons to tell me why I shouldn't even consider it.

Like most of the people around me at that time, I automatically thought that giving meant handing over money. Now, you may be a lot smarter than I was back then and you've probably worked out that there's a lot more than money you can give. That being said, listen carefully here, because there's something you can give that is not in any way "stuff" in the way we think of stuff. What that means is you can give something of enormous value that is not physical and will not cost you a dime. Before I share this, please remember that you may see no immediate external result of your contribution. However once you get into it, you will feel an immediate internal result.

So let me show you what I would do when I wanted to give but didn't feel I had the cash to do so. Imagine that you are in the car with me and I'm teaching you how to do this as we drive. We're in the car driving through downtown and as we drive, I ask you to pick out any person you see walking down the street. You point out a guy in a suit coming up on the right. At this point, I automatically put my inner focus on my heart area or heart center. I imagine love filling this entire area and when it's full (it might take a couple of seconds to feel this), I would imagine a beam of pure love and acceptance shooting out of my heart and pouring down onto this random person. After we drove past that person, you would point out another person and I'd repeat the process over and over with a new stranger every few seconds. After just a few of these "love shots," you would see that I am grinning from ear to ear. Now, I drive and you sit in the passenger seat. I ask you to get yourself centered and give it a go. You begin to focus on your heart, and you begin beaming out pure love and acceptance at all of these wonderful, nameless recipients. Within a few minutes, you too are grinning like Alice's proverbial Cheshire cat.

This is a wonderful, simple-to-do technique that will have you feeling abundantly blessed and generous within a very short period of time. In fact, I'll bet that even if you are feeling lower than a snake's belly and you go out and do this technique you'll still end up feeling fantastic in very short order. Perhaps you are wondering why do it while you driving, rather that while you are walking. You can do it while you walk too; I often do. However, it's good to do it while you drive or while you're on public transport looking out the window because it trains you to give without attachment. As you speed by, there's no way for you to check if the other person received your love and acceptance or not. So, yes, I recommend that you start off doing it while in a vehicle. The lesson here is that when we give without any attachment we end up getting far more than what we are giving. That, my friend, is what it means when you hear the phrase, "Give and it will come back to you a hundred fold."

The gift is in the giving! Does that make senses? So, come on, if you're reading this while someone is driving you or you're on public transit, give it a go. If not, put the book down for a second and look out of your window at some random passerby and shower them with all of your love and acceptance. I'm telling you, you'll feel great!

I'm willing to go out on a limb and say that when you get to the point in your consciousness, and as a result in your life, that you understand you can and do provide for and generate wealth, not just for yourself, but also for others. Then, you will know you have really made a quantum shift in consciousness with regards to what it takes to being in the flow of affluence and in turn becoming truly wealthy.

There are certain moments in every businessperson's life when they know they have stopped dabbling and are now in business. These are what I call "grown up business moments." Moments such as when you have to make a serious investment decision. It could be when you have to step up and fire someone. Another one of those moments is when you hire your first employee. When we first began to hire people to work with us in our company, one of our big goals was to assist them in creating wealth for themselves. We have said for years that are totally happy when we're writing big cheques. You see, we understand that for us to be writing big cheques to these individuals it's because they are also part of our wealth creation process. We understand that every cheque we write for them puts us deeper in the flow of affluence.

Listen, I know this might come as a shock but, it's a big fat "money myth" to think that the wealthy only think of themselves. The truly wealthy are not just thinking about how they can have more wealth. As pointed out earlier, a lot of the time they don't have to even think about it; it's pretty automatic. Many of the truly wealthy are thinking about how they can create wealth that extends far beyond themselves and even beyond their own families. This is, in fact, one of the key pieces in understanding not only wealth consciousness but also the flow of affluence that becomes wealth attraction.

You attract wealth not just because you are wealthy,
but because you are the generator of wealth for others.

~Dōv Baron

It's vitally important for you to realize that when you start generating within you and resonating out this kind of wealth consciousness, it becomes part of your quantum field, and it attracts people to you because your field energizes and excites their field. They may not even know why per se, but they will feel the pull and want to be part of what you are offering. Bear in mind, if you're reading this while still sitting in poverty consciousness then there's a good chance that your ego-mind flashed something like, *"What if they are attracted to it and then take it from me?"* Again, that's the difference between poverty or lack consciousness and affluent wealth consciousness. Wealth consciousness understands that for one person to have more, someone else doesn't have to have less.

Is this making senses? Are you really getting the feeling of how crucially imperative it is for you to make that shift, from "I can't. I don't have enough," into a place of genuine contribution? Just let yourself take a moment and write in your journal or in the margins of this book about how you can contribute and then make some kind of commitment to do so. It doesn't have to be some grand gesture. Remember the subconscious technique I taught you a few pages back? Just rain your love, acceptance, and deep feeling of affluence down on passersby—it feels soooooo gooood!

Before we move forward, there's one more thing that you will really want to let soak into very depth of your being. The truly wealthy are just as focused (if not more focused) on assisting others to become wealthy. Those who live in a lack mentality may find a way to generate wealth, but it will be joyless!

Now of course I'm going to ask you who do you need to go out there and share this with? Who else do you know who needs to get this? How many other people do you know that you need to put this knowledge in their hands, so that they can come out of the lack mentality which can suck the joy out of their lives?

All right, having made at least some level of shift in your understanding that you are now generating wealth that extends beyond you and as a result creates wealth for others, let's delve in a little deeper.

Chapter 18

Why You Can't Get Rich on Approval

How are you doing? Are you getting some powerful information? Are you applying at least some of it to create the financial transformation you want? I'll take that as a "yes." Okay, let's keep moving further forward and deeper into the subconscious realm.

Earlier I was saying that in your journey of moving away from lack and towards affluence, it's important to develop the courage to deal with the nay-sayers. What does that mean to you? Well here's a very important psychological fact that will help you deal with those thorn-in-the-foot kinds of folks. Most people, and when I say most I mean 99.9999 percent of people, carry a deep-seated fear of rejection. For most it's not a conscious thing. In fact, many people say things like, "I don't care what they think," but you know as well as I do that when-push-comes-to-shove, they care, big time. Let's face it, we all want to be liked and we all want to fit in with someone or something even if we're fitting in with others who don't fit in. This desire is rooted in basic human survival instincts, the safety of the tribe and such. However, the depth of this need to be connected to others is not supposed to be translated into what it so often becomes—a debilitating fear of rejection. Most of us were given the message by those who loved and took care of us that we must make sure people like us. *"Come on honey, smile for your uncle. You don't want him thinking you're miserable, do you? Be nice to the other kids or you won't have any friends."* It goes on and on. In and of themselves these are not "bad" messages; it's what we do with them that can become so crippling. We became programmed to seek acceptance because in our formative years we needed someone to take care of our every need. If someone didn't take care of you for the first few years of your life there's a good chance you wouldn't be reading this, right?

Here's the reason why understanding the fear of rejection is relevant to you when it comes to being in the flow of affluence and creating wealth in your life in such a way that it is not only significant but also lasting. Until you make a shift to thinking, feeling, and behaving in ways that are independent of the need to please others, you will never truly embrace following your heart and soul's passion, which is the key to tapping into your unique value. (Now, mentally hold onto those two words "unique value" because we will be addressing why those two words are pivotal to whether you are in or out of the flow of affluence.) Furthermore, if you do not develop the kind of independence I'm referring to, you can be pretty certain that true wealth will also evade you. Don't get me wrong. I am not suggesting that you become some thoughtless "a-hole" who doesn't care about anyone. No, this is about understanding that when you begin to follow your path, recognize your unique value, and make decisions based on that, money and wealth will flow to you. Once this begins to happen, you can also be fairly certain that you will, to put it plain and simple, begin to piss some folks off. I'll get into the why, in a little while.

As I'm sure you are beginning to see, if you don't move past the fear of rejection, getting what you really want will be impossible because, as the saying goes, you can't please all the people all the time. Being fixated on doing whatever it takes to not get rejected is nothing more than trying to please all the people all the time, with one exception; the one person you aren't pleasing—YOU!

Needless to say, it is crucial that you begin to destroy your fear of rejection. So how do you do that? Well, strangely enough you already know how, at least in some small way. It has to do with focusing your attention. When you are absolutely focused on what you are doing and how you are feeling while you are doing it, what others think doesn't matter. You no longer care if they are accepting or rejecting you. By becoming lost in what you are doing, by becoming completely engrossed, there is often the sense that what others think about you or your work just isn't important anymore.

Let me share an example with you.

> Carol had finally developed the courage to bring in the photographs. She had been saying that she would for over a month and it just never happened. She always had another excuse. Of course, I had called her on it over and over again and today was the day. She slipped her hand dubiously into the oversized leather briefcase and I could feel the trepidation as she slowly revealed the outside of the portfolio. It was no more than halfway out when she stopped and began explaining that it was all right if I didn't like the shots. She told me that I needed to remember that she was still learning and that she wouldn't be offended if I thought they were not very good.

"My God girl, you're setting me up to look at the ugliest photographs to have ever been taken in the history of the camera," I said.

"Well, I just don't want you to be disappointed," she said in a voice that transported a woman in her 50s back to being a small child.

"Did you take the photos for me?"

"No, I took them for myself, but I brought them in for you. I'd just as well not show them to you or anyone else."

"Are you sure about that? Are you sure you took them for yourself?"

"Yes, I'm sure." She said without conviction.

She was in the final stages of birthing the portfolio from the briefcase when I put my hand on top and stopped her. She was a little taken back, and lifting her eyes from their focus on the floor back to my eyes, she said with some surprise flavored with a dash of disappointment, "You don't want to see them now?"

"No, not now. I just want you to stop for a moment and without even looking at any of the photos, tell me about your favorite one."

Without missing a beat, her posture completely shifted, she sat more upright in her seat and said,

"That's got to be the ones of Jolie and her kitten." A soft smile lit her eyes as she spoke.

I leaned slightly forward and asked her to tell me what it felt like to be taking those photographs. She exhaled in a way that sounded like a soft sigh of relief. "It was wonderful. I hadn't planned taking shots of Jolie. I was just over visiting with my sister. Jolie is her daughter and obviously my niece. Anyway, my sister and I were in the kitchen having coffee and she'd been telling me about how Jolie just loved her new kitten." She continued, "My sister got up on her tip toes and began to sneak into the other room where Jolie was with the kitten. She laid her finger on her lips and said, "Shush," while motioning me to follow.

"I don't know why, but I automatically grabbed my camera and followed quietly along. Seconds later..."

Carol's face had now completely changed from the contorted tightness she had when she was going to show me the photographs to a completely soft child-like innocence.

She continued, "Seconds later, I had caught on film what was maybe one of the most unconditionally loving moments I have ever witnessed."

"Wow, that sounds beautiful."

"It was, it really was." Without any hesitation, Carol asked me, "Would you like to see those shots?"

"I would love to."

The photos of Jolie and the kitten were the last ones in the portfolio. It was as if she was either saving the best for last, hiding something precious or maybe both. The images were absolutely beautiful. Carol had caught something more than a red haired, very cute kid cuddling with a kitten. She had, as she so very well articulated, caught an act of unconditional love on film for all to see.

She kindly shared the rest of her photographs with me and they were all quite beautiful. She clearly had an artist's eye and could envision things in a way that most of us would have missed. About half way through looking at the shots I stopped and asked Carol a question that I believed changed the way she saw what her photography was about. "Do you re-member how shy you were about showing me the photographs when you first came in today?"

"Yes, of course I do. I was terrified that you would hate them and think I was just no good at this."

It was at that point that I hit her with the question that rearranged her matrix. "When you were watch-ing your niece with the kitten and you were taking those shots, did you ever once think about my opin-ion or for that matter anyone else's?"

"No, of course not, I was lost in the moment. I was taking them for me."

"And in that moment how did it feel to be taking the photos for yourself."

Her one word answer shocked her: "Free." Once she said it, we both sat there silently for many seconds because there was nothing else to say. She had gotten it.

Carol's story is a great illustration of what I was saying about finding the courage to stand up to the nay-sayers because most of the time the nay-sayers live in your head. They are the old conditioned limiting beliefs we talked about a few chapters back; old beliefs that have never been questioned and held as truth without supporting evidence. Giving in to the public opinion of what is right, wrong, good, or bad not only robs you, but also the world of the precious gift that is your unique value set.

Is this making senses? I do hope so. I hope that one hit you right in the soft parts because I know with all certainty you have something to offer the world that's bigger than what you have been offering.

Let yourself feel what would happen if you stepped up your game. How would you like to hold the keys to financial abundance and true prosperity? *Imagine Multiplying Your Prosperity With Ease!*

Set yourself free from the fear by releasing the idea that they might reject you. So what if they do! Those who would reject you for doing what you are passionate about are not people who truly care enough to honor your path. By setting yourself free, you will tap into the most powerful tool available for generating a resonance of power, passion, and prosperity so that you become a magnet for success.

Picture yourself smiling with calm confidence as you become immune to the negativity of others scurrying around in confused panic over their finances. Let yourself feel it now!

As we discussed earlier, fear is one the biggest blocks between you and the success you desire. You get that now, right?

Just for a moment, if you want to, imagine how unstoppable you would be if those limiting beliefs that have generated all your fears were gone. Can you imagine how that would impact the quality of your relationships, the quality of your health, and of course the quality of your finances? Look. I wrote this book for a whole list of great reasons, not least of all my desire to empower you to know that you are capable of having and being far more than "they" have told you.

As I've stated on numerous occasions money isn't the answer to all your problems. However, not having it and constantly struggling isn't either.

Our philosophy is that this world needs more affluent people with a soul. We need more people who deeply care about those around them and the world in general. The question is, "Are you willing to take a few simple, actionable steps to be one of the elite few that do?"

Listen, if you really want to step up your game and actually take control of what's showing up in your life may I suggest you attend Claim Your Competitive Edge™ live event. It is three days of absolutely ego-mind blowing knowledge and experiences. What's more, as a reward for buying this book I'm giving you two tickets to attend this event. That's a value of $1,600 as my gift to you, because you have shown a genuine commitment to raising your consciousness and being in the flow of affluence.

I've got to tell you that Claim Your Competitive Edge™ is one of the most upbeat and lively experiential events you'll ever attend and at the same time, the amount of knowledge and experience you'll gain will propel you to new heights in your life, your relationships and of course your finances. Claim Your Competitive Edge™ is immersive and experiential— you'll get to do some really cool things that you never thought possible.

Claim Your Competitive Edge™ will give you the competitive edge without losing your soul!

Throughout this chapter, we've talked a lot about how important it is to deal with the fears that block you. Well, when you attend the Claim Your Competitive Edge™ event, you will walk out having completely crushed your three biggest fears…Guaranteed!

Right here I'm giving you the secret to be able to attend this life-changing event as my guest. http://www.CYCEdge.com/drtmb

As I said, when you shift your resonance field you can, be, do and have what you had only previously imagined!

Making senses? Great, let's keep moving because the bottom line is if you're not having the kind of success you dream of in any particular area of your life it's worth asking yourself: Who do I fear will reject me if I fully embrace my success in this area?

It is this fear of rejection that keeps the brakes on while your desire is to push on the gas pedal. Living your life looking over your shoulder as if someone is just waiting to reject you, is not only a little paranoid, but it creates an environment that does not facilitate creativity—and creativity is essential for true wealth consciousness.

Chapter 19

The Power of Consequences

In the last chapter, we discussed that one of the great walls blocking people from achieving their most desired outcomes in life is their fear of rejection. Let's look at another one of the hurdles that can stand in the way of you positioning yourself directly in the flow of affluence and abundance, and more importantly, what you can do to not only get over, but destroy that hurdle.

In an earlier chapter I was explaining to you that the one thing that all long-term successfully wealthy individuals have is wealth consciousness. As a consequence of having this level of wealth consciousness, they do things differently than the average person does who is stuck in a job they don't like. Might I suggest that as you go through the rest of the book you really take a look at applying into your life some of the empowering behaviors of these individuals? Allow me to give you a peek behind the curtain so that you can take a look at one of the most distinguishing behaviors of the truly wealthy.

If you really want to be able to embrace success and wealth at your dream level, you need to be able to make fast and accurate decisions on whatever is in front of you. Hold on, before you go running for the hills screaming like a banshee, I realize that even saying such a thing can be an out for some people's ego-minds, causing their inner voice to scream something like *I'm no good at decisions, so that's just never going to happen for me.* This, of course, is the old ego-mind doing its job of insisting that who you were is all you'll ever be, and by now you know that's a load of horse fertilizer.

What I mean when I say that you have to be able to make fast and accurate decisions on whatever is in front of you is that you must be able to recognize extraordinary opportunities when they are presented. This is something that the truly successful are extremely good at. You see they have been trained or have trained themselves to recognize opportunity whenever it is on the horizon. They are operating out of the flow of affluence that's coming from having wealth consciousness; they are attracting these opportunities at every turn.

Instead of asking, "Where can I find an opportunity?" the truly successful, the truly wealthy are wondering which opportunity to take advantage of first, in any economy. These kind of individuals quickly evaluate the risk and the opportunity that's in front of them. They understand they need to act now, while at the same time they want as much relevant information as they can get before deciding. There's a saying in business: The highly successful make decisions quickly and change their minds slowly. While I'll be the first to say how important it is to listen to your intuition, please note that listening to your intuition does not mean jumping into the first idea that pops in your head. At the same time, listening to intuition is not about anal-izing the opportunity until it's drained of its life force.

Think about what that means? Better still think about what that could mean if you now began applying it. Needless to say, coming at an opportunity from this point of view means that you are going to see things that others would have just missed; things that, in all likelihood, the old you would have missed.

What are the Consequences?

How do you go about putting this in place? It can be quite simple. You start by doing an overall analysis of what's possible and then you ask yourself, "What can I get from this? What might truly be in this for me?" Remember though, this is your starting point. We're not done yet; we don't want you going off half-cocked, do we?

Once you've got the upside clear you need to be really honest in relation to the real risk/cost, because, and listen to me on this one: Everything, no matter how good it seems, has a cost and/or potential negative consequence. Just for the record, at this point I think it's always a good idea to bring in someone you really trust, but not someone you trust just because they always agree with you. Once you have truly looked at the risk ratio and they've weighed in, you can make your decision. Again, this is not something you need to anal-ize for the next hundred years.

Here's something that may shock some folks. There is no real governing body that can stop you from doing whatever it is that you choose to do. Did you get that? I mean did you really get it? Do us both a favor and go back and read that sentence again. I know there are all kinds of teachers and gurus who will tell you that you are free to do anything as long as it doesn't hurt or infringe on others. Whether that's true or not, what you want to be certain about is this: You can do *whatever* you choose to, anything at all, as long as you are willing to pay the price.

Where I grew up, that translated to:
Don't do the crime if you can't do the time.

Living in the kind of environment that I grew up in, that quote rattled around in my head for most of my adolescence. It kept me on the right side of the law because I knew I had taken the time to realize I didn't have any desire to do the time. So while many of the people I knew were committing crimes, I stayed straight, not because I was better or more moral than them, but because I was honest with myself about the risk/consequences that I was and was not willing to take.

What's fascinating about this was that as I looked at where I was living as a child and accessed the risk-return on leaving my familiar environment and traveling, I did so with very little hesitation. My peers stayed put. They just couldn't live with the consequences of leaving their safe environment behind. It doesn't make my decision right and theirs wrong vice versa; it simply means that each of us must evaluate our own risk-return ratio in direct relation to what we want and the price we are willing to pay to get it. To say it again, the bottom line is that you can have whatever you desire as long as you are willing to pay the price. And to reiterate, the questions worth asking, the questions that are so rarely asked are:

- Have you honestly accessed the "real" price of what you desire?

- Are you actually willing to pay that price?

I've been in business for many years and, as you can imagine, there are many upsides to being in business for yourself. However, as anyone who's ever been in business can tell you, there are also many down-sides. Over the years, I've met many people who want to get out of their **J.O.B.**s (just-over-broke) and start their own business. They tell me they are ready and although I think that it's great and I believe that you must start your own business if you are ever going to experience financial freedom, in my experience very few people know what it really means to go into business. Being in business for yourself does not, at least initially, mean working fewer hours. It will, without doubt, mean working many more hours and doing without the overtime pay you might get from an employer. Please note, I'm not saying that you'll have to give up your family or all of your free time. It is about understanding that if you go into business for yourself, I would highly recommend that you focus on something you absolutely love, because you will be investing more than just your money. I'll go into more about this in the next chapter, but for now, just know that having your own business is not for wimps! It is however, ideal for those who have the courage and determination to express their heart and soul's desire to be an active creative force in the world.

So, bringing it back to the bare bones, before you jump in to something, ask yourself if you can live with the ultimate negative consequence if all goes wrong. As I said, this has been a powerful guiding line, not just in business but across the board in my life. While it has guided me, at the same time it has not stopped from willing to do things that many considered too risky for them.

Having done your assessment of possible consequences, if you can live with the risk ratio of the potential downside consequences paired against the upside consequences, then this is an opportunity you can embrace. That is what a risk ratio is all about and those who are truly wealthy know this. Here's the challenge. Your ego-mind's overriding prime directive is to be right, even if that means being right about not getting it right. (There's a mind twister for you!) It's for that reason we don't want you to just jump into something without looking at the potential positive and negative consequences. As a generality the ego-mind tends to say "no" to the opportunities that show up because it wants to keep things the same. Saying "yes" means taking a chance on something less predictable which is not the ego-mind's favorite choice.

When it comes to living a rich and fulfilling life, if your ego-mind has been running the show, you will discover that the challenge will be a tendency towards saying "no" pretty much automatically. However, life only gets exciting and fulfilling when we are willing to say "yes." This doesn't mean polarizing your ego-mind's automatic "no" with an automatic "yes." What it means is that it's okay to say "maybe, just give me a minute" until you have honestly done enough research with regard to the risk management. Putting this as simple as possible, you don't say "yes" or "no" until you have gathered enough information to say your answer with certainty.

We have been talking here about recognizing opportunity when it shows up and having a process for actually recognizing the distinction between an opportunity and an opportunity *that's right for you*. Keep in mind that an opportunity is not an opportunity if you are not interested. And an opportunity is not an opportunity if it's out of synch with your own core values.

I'm about to get quite intimate with you, I trust that you'll be okay with that? I'm choosing to do this because I want you to really understand that one of my clear guidelines for myself as a teacher is to not ask you to do what I would not do myself—it's a matter of integrity for me.

> On a clear sunny afternoon in the June of 1990, I was free climbing a rock face in British Columbia, Canada. I had been working like a crazy man going backwards and forwards across the United States and Canada, and a spot of camping flavored with a large dose of adrenaline seemed to be the perfect recreational remedy. At around 120 feet up I reached for a rock. The rock dislodged a bigger rock that hit me in the face knocking me unconscious and sending me down to the jagged boulders below at maximum velocity. As you can imagine,

I was seriously injured. Without going into what are some very gory details, I will tell you that the physical, mental, and emotional recovery process was very long and demanding. Within a matter of moments, I went from being a fairly successful speaker making a very decent income to being on disability. Times were hard and there came a period when more than anything I wanted to get back on my feet and begin speaking again. Sadly, at that time, (pre-Internet) that would take money and I didn't have much more than a survival income. To make extra money I worked nights in a 24-hour gym. I've worked out since I was in my late teens so it seemed like a reasonable fit for me. The work was menial and mindless but I got to meet some very interesting people, some of whom even became my friends.

On one particular day at around 3 AM when my eyes were burning with fatigue, one of the regular late night workout guys came in and, as usual, began to chat with me. He started out by massaging my ego a little, saying stuff about how I seemed to be in the wrong job and that I seemed too smart to be working nights in a gym, tidying up weights and making protein shakes. He asked me what I was doing before working at the gym and I filled him in on my speaking background and the fact that I had fallen off a mountain.

He suddenly looked very perky and said with a great deal of certainty, "I think I can help you."

"Really, how's that?" I asked with genuine curiosity.

"Well, it seems to me that if you had some money you could get back to work at making a difference in people's lives."

"Go on, I'm listening." He definitely had my attention.

"How much do you need to get going?"

I honestly had no idea and told him so, but the fact that he was asking brought up a combination of suspicion and wanting to believe that he was some kind angel investor.

"Well, what if I gave you an opportunity to make between a half and one million dollars in a year working for me?"

As I said, I've not been a fan of the J.O.B. thing, but this was sounding good and even I could have put up with a boss for a year if it meant making a cool million. Let's face it, a million bucks had a lot more buying power back in the early nineties. I began thinking about how I could make enough money in just one year to completely launch my career again. This was very enticing! With reasonably healthy caution I asked, "How do I even know this is for real?"

He was very cool when he looked me in the eyes and asked, "Have you seen the cars I drive?" I had and they (plural) were very nice.

"Have you seen my jewelry?" I personally have no pull towards such things, but I can see when something is real or just has the "bling effect." His was definitely real.

"Have you seen how many hot chicks I have following me around?" Each night there would be a new one.

I said nothing, waiting for him to finish.

"These things are real, and so is my offer." Now I have to tell you that I didn't particularly like this guy before. I had never been particularly impressed by his "stuff," but the idea of being able to jump start my dream within a year and having what for me at the time would have been a big pile of cash was very appealing.

"Okay, I'm listening, what's the job?"

Calm, cool and collected, he leaned over the counter at me and said, "I will wholesale to you. You find runners who will sell the product for you. I get paid up front after the first month, which I will front for you. Your runners make a couple of bucks on each transaction and you make the big profits."

I have to tell you that as tempting as it was, as much as my ego-mind could justify any action in the name of later on being able to make a difference in people's lives, the idea of selling drugs, even as a wholesaler, just didn't work for me. Even though I have no judgment on those who choose to use them, I knew being a dealer was out of the question for me. It was in direct conflict with my higher values. On top of that, I knew I couldn't do the time. The conversation ended when I turned his offer down.

As a consequence of my values-based decision, it did take me considerably longer to get on my feet. The fact that night after night this guy would pull up in his shiny new car with another "hottie" hanging off of his arm didn't help reduce the second-guessing or feeling the temptation to try it his way. I understand that for some of you, it would have been a clean-cut, easy decision to make. However, until any of us are faced with a particular situation in a particular context, none of us can ever be absolutely certain what we would even consider doing or not doing.

Over the next eighteen or so months, almost every time I hit the financial wall my ego-mind would jump in with some kind of *I told ya so* message. However, as difficult as it was to turn my back on the money, I was able to go about my life without looking over my shoulder or compromising my integrity. And within the following two years I was back on my feet doing what I do to assist other people in discovering their own inner strength. In fact, it was about two years later that I received a call from a guy I had met during that time. It appeared that he had taken the "opportunity" I had turned down and he was looking to come and see me for some counseling. The following week he arrived for his appointment in, well you guessed it, a nice shiny new SUV. He walked into my office with a swagger of confidence and within the first five minutes, he had become the external verification that my late night decision had been an excellent one. He had started out in the business and made himself a promise that he would not use the product. He had gone on to make a lot of money and he had all the toys and a party life. However, what started out as a bending of the rules a little had become a full-blown addiction. Where he went from there is not particularly relevant to where we are going in this book. His story is a reminder of what can happen when you fail to follow your truth. However, when, in spite of the temptation to do otherwise, you are honest with yourself, you will in time, if you pay attention, receive validation of your self-trust.

What I'm simply saying is there will always be opportunities. You just have to have a high level of self-honesty, examine whatever is being offered in order to weigh the risk ratio. In my case, the drug wholesaling business had a very low risk ratio when it came to financial profit and loss. This guy was willing to front me the first month's supply. I wouldn't have been out on the street dealing with shady characters. I would just have had a few guys to deal with and loads of cash coming back. On the surface, it all looks pretty good on the risk ratio scale. However, the real risk for me was the abandonment of my higher values.

I trust that this is making senses? Just let yourself feel the truth of it. When you are operating from a place of affluence, you will recognize an opportunity whenever it is on the horizon. Just let yourself deeply know that coming at an opportunity from this point of view means that you are going to see things that others would have just missed; things that, in all likelihood, you would have missed if and when you were in a lack mentality.

Notice what happens within you when you truly let these two ideas sink into your subconscious being: recognizing opportunities when they show up, and having a process for recognizing the distinction between an opportunity and an opportunity that's right for you.

Remember, an opportunity is not an opportunity if it's out of synch with your own core values. That being said, you will need to monitor the ego-mind because it will even use made-up core values as an excuse to avoid moving forward..

Just for a moment, sit up in your chair, take another deep breath out, and then in again. With that breath coming in, feel the certainty of being able to evaluate quickly the risk and the opportunity that's in front of you. How quickly would your life and the circumstances around it shift in the direction of your dreams if you now let that happen? Let yourself remember that *the highly successful make decisions quickly and change their minds slowly*.

Having said that, I want to move on to looking at the biggest opportunity you could ever be offered—the opportunity that is you...

Chapter 20

Getting Them to Bang Down Your Door to Give You Money

Wouldn't it be great if you could get people to bang down your door and give you their money? Imagine how amazing that would feel! Let's face it, if that was happening, you would be absolutely certain that you had the competitive edge, right? Well, let's see what we can do about giving you that edge.

Getting them to bang down your door to give you money is all about two things:

     1) Finding and tapping into your unique value
     2) Offering that value to others

Simple, right?
Well yes, on the surface. So let's go below the surface.

To create true abundance in your life you will need both an external and an internal process. By now you beginning to understand that having an external experience of abundance, (money in your pocket or bank account), is a direct result of living an internal

173

experience of abundance (what's going on with you at the level of thoughts, feelings and beliefs). Let's just think about this for a moment. As much as we may like to consider ourselves as fairly enlightened, we also know that, to some degree, the internal experience is simulated, and at least to some degree determined by the external experience.

It goes something like this: Wealthy thinking/feeling/believing (internal) = wealthy experiences; money and stuff, (external). Having money and stuff gives us the validation of experiencing abundance and creates the thinking, feeling and believing. The beliefs generate a thought process and, in turn, feelings then build within us (internal) and add to our quantum resonance field, attracting more of the external experiences that validate us (external).

I know that might seem a bit difficult to get your head around, but give it another read. Because when you do get it, you'll see that it's a loop that flows in both directions.

Put simply:
Being leads to having, and having leads to being.

What you want to understand is that this process is a loop. You must have both internal and external experiences going on in order to believe, attract, and maintain the flow of abundance because one feeds into the other repeating the cycle over and over again. However, in this section of the book I want to focus on your getting the external result because I've already been giving you a great start with the internal, which I will come back to a little later.

Side Bar: *If you really want assistance with the very best internal process technology, have a look at:* http://www.EquationForManifestation.com

On many occasions throughout this book, I have stressed that real wealth is a lot more than money. In fact, money is only one expression of wealth. Nonetheless, it can be an important part of the whole experience.

Now here's where you will want to sit up straight and really pay attention because what I'm about to share is critically important in the process of creating real wealth. The challenge is that your ego-mind could easily respond with *"Oh yeah, I know that. It's obvious."* My warning to you is do not go there. This is simple, but not without a multitude of layers to its understanding. Simply put:

***If you want to create wealth in your life,
you've got to be able to recognize value.***

More specifically, you must be able to recognize your own value.

It's by delivering value that all wealth is created. It's by delivering your own unique brand of value that you will naturally create your own wealth.

If you are genuinely resonating from a place of abundance, then you are in the flow of affluence and opportunities will present themselves to you at every turn. However, if you cannot recognize value, when those opportunities show up you will, in all likelihood, miss them entirely. Moreover, if you have nothing of your own that has value to offer anyone else, why would anyone give you their money? ***Remember, money is nothing more than an energetic medium of exchange!***

What I'm about to share with you is the true secret to understanding and creating abundance; it is one of the great competitive edges. Perhaps you believe that going out and buying "stuff" is imortant.

Perhaps you even believe that the value you offer in exchange for money means stuff, but the fact is that people buy energy, whether it's your personal energy in the form of a service you offer or your energy expressed through the product you create. People are always buying the experience of being in, or connected to, your energy.

Did you get that? Just think about it for a moment and you'll see it really makes senses.

Let me illustrate with a story.

> Several years ago, I was out tootling around with a friend who was picking up some groceries. I have to admit that I am not typically the kind of person who notices the price of something. In fact, as I'm writing this I just thought to myself *"What's the price of a loaf of bread or a carton of milk?"* The honest truth is I don't have a clue. Anyway, I'm out with this friend when she goes into her local store and picks some basic groceries. To be clear, this local grocery store is in one of the more trendy parts of town. She selected a particular item, which, because I had happened to buy the exact same thing that morning in a regular mega supermarket, I noticed was double the price I had paid.

> I innocently said, "You do know you could get that for less than half that price at the mega store, right?"

> She was very calm and equally certain in her response, "I would happily pay twice, even three times as much here than go there."

"Why's that?" I said feeling somewhat confused.

"Look around," she said, taking in the clean natural light flowing in through big windows instead of the florescent blinking that was part of big box shopping store. Rather than a muffled voice that would interrupt bad muzak with a message that there was need for clean up on aisle five, spa-type music was playing softly in the background. The scent of freshly baked goods from the whole grain bakery floated throughout the store. "Do you see crowds of people banging into each other for the special price on laundry detergent?" Before I could answer she went on, "Do you see any check-out people who look like they would rather be anywhere else than here?" I looked toward the checkout and all the people serving actually looked quite happy. "Dōv, I don't just come here for groceries. I come here because this is part of my community and I am happy to pay more to support my community."

I know she said her reasons for shopping there were about community, but the truth is that statement was nothing more than the justification she needed for being in the energy that the storeowner had set up. She and a good many other people were happy to pay a premium price to experience that energy. Remember:

Nothing is ever bought or sold beyond the desire for an experience we hope that energy will bring.

The owner of that store fully understood *that* truth—even if it was at a subconscious level—remained their competitive edge.

Let me give you another great example of a company that clearly and deliberately understands this. This is a company that, in all likelihood, you have had a firsthand experience of being in their energy.

When you think about Starbucks™ purely from the position of money exchanged for a product, there was every reason for them to fail. When they started out, they sold coffee at about four times the price of their competitors. Imagine sitting down with your friends and saying, *"Yeah, I'm going to open a business and I'm going to sell pretty much the same thing as the guy down the street except I'm going to charge about four times more for it."* What do you imagine your friends would think of that idea?

The obvious question is, "Why would anyone pay so much for a cup of coffee?" The simple answer is that Starbucks™ has never sold "coffee." What they sell is the energetic experience of what they call "the third place experience."

Starbucks™ wants you to think of their store as the third place you'd hang out at, with the first being home, and the second being work. The Starbucks™ third place philosophy is similar to that of NBC TV's longest running sitcom, "Cheers," the place where everyone knows your name as well as your beverage of choice. Starbucks™ management understands this, so they train their staff to do what it takes so that you have an experience of their store being your third place.

Do you get it? Everything we purchase, we purchase because we want an experience and there is energy to that experience.

That being said:

- What do you have to offer?

- What is the unique value you bring to the world that people will line up at your door to give you money for?

When you know and apply this, you, my friend, will have a competitive edge that's as potentially successful in your niche as Starbucks™ is in theirs. If you don't know the answer, it's because you are blind (as are most people) to your own gifts. Right now, I want to reward you for getting this far in this book with an exercise that will assist you in getting clear about the unique value you offer. Now let me be honest, you can skip right over this exercise, you can tell yourself that you'll deal with it later, which we both know is highly unlikely, or you can actually embrace it as a gift by taking it on and doing what you now need to do to discover your unique value. The choice is yours…

Okay, ready? Get out a pen and paper and write down the names of five people who know you well. Go on—I'm not going anywhere. Done it? Okay, now write down the names of another five people who know you, but not as well as the first five.

Got your lists? I'll assume yes.

Now here's the next step. Make a commitment to call or meet with each of the folks on both lists over the next seven days. (If you spread it out too far it's easy to become disconnected from what was said.) Ask each of them to be totally honest and tell you what they see as your greatest gifts and strengths. Then ask each of them to tell you what they see as your "personal genius blind spot." This means the area in which you have a level of brilliance that you either take for granted or just don't see. Take down every word you hear, even if you have no interest in pursuing it, even if you think the person is completely wrong, crazy or on something.

Next, collect the data, sift through it and look for common themes. Why? Because this, my friend, is GOLD! Do not waste this information because the key to the treasure chest is now in your hands.

All you've got to do is put it in action. You see, once you have collected your data and sorted out the common themes, you can apply the principle of "unique value" by designing a product or service around what came out of your survey. What you come up with will be an expression of your inner genius, your unique value set. That, my friend, is the energy the world wants. Once you've found your unique value set, people will happily be banging down your door to give you their money to get some of it.

Let me summarize this into a nutshell so that it makes real senses to you: To have a consistent experience of affluent flow in your life you must first have an internal representation of it. If you can't see it/ feel it on the inside, it's not likely to show up on the outside in your bank account. Does that make senses? Okay, that being said, you will need to have some kind of evidence for what has been internally represented in order to hold the belief. The good news is, the more you notice whatever level of affluence/flow that shows up, the more of it you receive.

Just sit there for a moment and contemplate that loop cycle and how it shows up in your life. Just let yourself feel into it because it works both ways. If a person has been running a ton of lack thinking, feeling and believing, then they are likely noticing more and more of that in their outer reality and as a result that loop cycle is bringing them more of what they say they don't want. Here's one of my favorite sayings that can really help you wrap your head around this:

The mind is constantly looking for evidence of what it believes to be true, even if what it believes is completely false.

Put in the simplest form—your ego-mind has blinders on. Just let yourself become aware of what happens within you as you let that soak in. It's pretty amazing, isn't it? Detect who was the first person who popped into your mind that you need to share this with, and go share it with them. Not only will it enrich their lives, it will allow you to keep getting the meaning of this chapter on a deeper level yourself.

Did you really let yourself take in the deeper meaning of what I was sharing about value?

You will recollect I was saying that if you want to create wealth in your life, you've got to be able to recognize value. More specifically you must be able to recognize your own unique value set. It is by delivering value that all wealth is created. It is by delivering your own unique brand of value that you will naturally create wealth. That took us to the exercise I designed to assist you in discovering "your unique value set" and get underneath what had been your "genius blind spots."

Honestly, just stop and check in with yourself, and discover how great you could feel right now about discovering your own "unique value set." Imagine making your affluent flow of finances by doing something that is totally natural to you, something you love and that people would be willing to bang down your door to be able to have.

In any kind of business the secret is finding a need in the market place and being able to uniquely fill it, because you will be compensated by how well you fill that need.

I'm going to take you deeper into your Unique Value Set in the next chapter, so stay with me.

Sidebar:
Book Bonus: For more on creating the resonance to really attract what you want...**I'm giving you 5 FREE video lessons into some of**

the most overlooked ingredients of successful manifestation.

To take a look and register to receive these lessons go over to:
http://www.EquationForManifestation.com

Chapter 21

Your Unique Value Set...
The Path to Infinite Riches

Are you excited? If you did the exercise at the end of the last chapter, you have every right to be. I want you to stay connected to that excitement while, at the same time, it's very important that you stay grounded. So with that in mind, let's start by understanding that there are two sides to your unique value. One side is what you already have, what you already know, what you can already, do and in many ways, what is already inherently part of you. (Remember, as you learned in the last exercise I gave you, even though you already have whatever it is that you have, you may not have been able to see or recognize it.) The other piece of your unique value is the part that your ego-mind can use to pull you off track. You will discover that part over time as a natural expansion of your evolution; it just might take years and years.

In an effort to keep you grounded and at the same time get you going in the right direction, we aren't going to be looking into any crystal balls. Instead, we'll stick with what you already have because that's what you can tap into right here right now.

Earlier I talked a little about "money myths." One of these is that being wealthy is all about who you know. In reality, people are the holders of the wealth you are looking to tap into. However, if you have nothing to offer them why would they pass their money on to you? It certainly doesn't do any harm for you to have some great contacts, but if you don't have the consciousness to hold the wealth, (or wealthy connection) they will just go away.

Let me put it to you this way: What if you already have the contacts and connections and resources you need to be as successful as you desire to be? I ask you that question for the simple purpose of bringing you back to what I just said—your unique value is about what you already have! In looking for your unique value, one thing will become evident: Much of your value is something you take for granted.

Come with me. I'm going to take a little side excursion here because I think it will truly help you understand why you may have been blind to, or at least taken for granted, what you have as unique value. As a generality, do you know many people who jump out of bed with excitement to go to work each morning? The truth is that very few people see work as a joy. In fact, many people refer to work as a four letter word that they just have to do in order to pay the bills.

Now let me ask you, do you have a friend or have you ever met someone who is extraordinarily talented at something they do as a hobby and they won't take money for it? This person would literally spend every waking moment doing the thing they love if they didn't have other obligations—like work. All too often, that same super talented person goes to work each day in a job they don't like for money to pay the bills.

Why is that?

One word answer: Conditioning!

We have all been trained to believe that if it's fun we somehow shouldn't get paid for it. We should only be paid for being miserable. Let me tell you something: I am a blessed man. I get up each morning and go to work in a career that I adore. But you know what is absolutely insane? Because of societal conditioning many people think that because I work in something I love and because my work is for the betterment of mankind, I am supposed to just give away my value and I should just do my work for free.

Let me tell you something. It's not my intention to be mean, rude or without compassion for someone's particular circumstances; my purpose is just to give it to you straight up. Anyone who is carrying around that kind of thinking is, without doubt, financially broke. They have a poverty consciousness based on poverty beliefs and, I'm sorry to say that, as long as they are committed to those kinds of beliefs, they will always be in financial struggle. Are you with me here?

Real wealth comes to those who love what they do! As I started out saying, the only thing anyone ever sells is energy. People line up to give them big fat wads of cash just to get close to that energy, to that level of love, in action.

So back to discovering your unique value set...

What do you know more about than the average person does? A big clue here is that your ego-mind will tell you that "everyone knows that" and it's a freakin liar. Just because you know it, does not mean everyone knows it and even if they did, it's very unlikely that they know about it in the way that you do.

I remember a great story from one of my favorite metaphysical teachers from the eighties, Stuart Wilde. I'll do my best to tell the story as I remember it:

> Years ago a friend of Stuart's, who most considered less than a particularly bright fellow, would go to the movies with Stuart and some other mates and drive them all crazy. You see on every occasion that they were watching a war movie, (there seemed to be a lot at that time), this guy would get irritated that the German soldier had his hat on wrong. He griped that the vehicle in a particular scene wasn't put into production until two years after the time in which this scene was set. He took great pains to point out every mistake to those around him and, of course, ruined the movie for everyone in earshot.

> You see, this guy was fascinated with World War II memorabilia and he knew stuff that very few people on the planet knew, for that matter, he knew stuff very few people couldn't care less about. Anyway, as I remember the story, one day this guy's mates got sick of his moaning and complaining and told him to stop telling them and start telling the movie companies. Upon hearing this advice, he did something very rare. He listened. He wrote to the studios saying that the soldier in this particular scene had his hat on wrong and that some of the equipment in the scene didn't fit with the time period of the movie.

> Apparently, his letter reached the right person because he was invited to consult on an upcoming

movie. Within a short period of time, this guy was the lead technical historian for a big movie company. Now here's the rather lovely twist: With all the money he made, he traveled the world buying World War II memorabilia, which he would then lease, to the movie companies for a very handsome fee on top of his equally handsome consulting fee. Not bad for a guy whose mates thought to be a bit thick.

What's the difference between this guy and you? The answer is *very little*. He was, with the help of friends, able to recognize his unique value set and then he took action. So once again I ask you: What's the unique value set you have that you haven't seen or have taken for granted?

Maybe you're still thinking, *I don't have any special skills or knowledge.* Come on, just stop the mind chatter for a couple of minutes and think about your life experiences. You will find a banquet of unique values right there. Maybe you've been sick with a particular illness your entire life. Well, then you know a lot more about being sick than the average person and you certainly know more than the person who has just discovered that they are sick with that illness. Listen, very often it's our adverse situations, the places in our lives where we feel the most challenged that are the metaphorical UPS/Fed Ex of our unique value set.

Take my friend Annie Hopper. Annie started out as a stock trader on Toronto's Bay Street. She spent nine years in what she calls an "adrenaline junkie's" dream job and working in an environment that she describes as nothing less than "soul sucking." Finally, she decided she'd had enough and changed careers. Since she wanted a less adrenaline-based lifestyle, she trained to become a registered massage therapist.

With her schooling completed, she packed her bags and moved to the West coast. Being Annie, she really took on the idea of being genuinely relational. Because she operates out of that mindset, she is an amazing people connector. Within a short time, she started and successfully operated her own massage therapy practice in Vancouver, Canada and successfully did so for twelve years. By this time, you can see that Annie had not only left a career and a lifestyle, but as a result, new curiosity had been awakened within her. She became fascinated with how mental stress and emotional health relates to the physical body.

It was at this time that I met Annie. It seems that someone she was working on had told her about the work I do and that it fit strongly with that inner pull she was feeling. Once again, the career ground was already beginning to shift beneath her feet. There was a pull within her and at that point, she was where most of us have been at one time or another; knowing that she had to leave behind what she had, while not knowing where she was going. Annie became committed to her own growth and development and studied under me for a couple of years and then went on to become a counselor certified in life coaching.

Things appeared to be bubbling along; her career as a life coach became very successful. She had her own weekly column in a newspaper and was featured on a local talk radio station. Annie had been enormously courageous in following her path without ever really knowing where it would take her and I've always admired that about her. What she did hold onto as a certainty was that there's some reason behind whatever was going on and she trusted that she would find it.

As successful as Annie would become, nothing prepared her for what was to come next. Let me just say that if you were having a social event and you knew Annie, you would want her there. She was warm, friendly, and funny, and over the years she had truly developed a sense of herself that gave this barely five feet tall woman a big presence. She loved getting together with friends for chats, martinis, laughs, and even a spot of dancing. Then in 2005, Annie developed some strange symptoms that seemed to come out of nowhere and for no apparent reason. Looking back, she could see that they started with severe insomnia and a sudden and unusual increased sensitivity to scented products like perfumes, colognes, fabric softeners, deodorizers, and strongly scented cleaning agents. However, on their own, each of these symptoms made no sense.

Over the next year, the symptoms severely escalated. Annie was suddenly having seizure-like reactions when she was around things like a cordless phone or computer. You and I may never notice that we are surrounded by chemicals every single day. However, for Annie, everyday chemicals from things like personal hygiene products or laundry detergent would send her into a total tailspin. Her body would go into a severe aversion response. This occurs when your body reacts as if your very life is being threatened. She would experience piercing headaches that were a fifteen on the one to ten pain intensity scale. She would lose her ability to speak, become confused and disoriented. Her heart would go into rapid palpitations, her body would flush, she would cry uncontrollably and even go into convulsions at times. Fun, social Annie was quickly disappearing as if she was being consumed from the inside out by something that no one was initially able to even label, let alone treat.

She eventually discovered that in 2005 she had developed what is known as Environmental Illness or Multiple Chemical Sensitivities (MCS). By 2007, the sensitivity had expanded and she had also developed Electrical Sensitivities on top of chemical sensitivities. MCS and Electrical Sensitivities are caused from an acquired brain injury that impairs limbic system function and triggers a conditioned immune response. (Among its other functions, the limbic system manages the hormones that generate the "fight or flight" response.) As a result, MCS and EI can be the cause of chronic fatigue syndrome, fibromyalgia, anxiety disorders, chronic pain syndromes, and depression. As you can imagine this was devastating for Annie and the Annie everyone had come to know and love.

At its worst, Annie became homeless, living in a campground because her body could not tolerate any of the chemicals or electromagnetic fields that were part of her own home. Like a dog that howls at a noise you and I cannot hear, she could hear electricity as a piercing hum. Her sense of smell and taste became something befitting of a character developed in Hollywood, heightened to detect the slightest amount of chemicals in any product. If she encountered someone who had laundered their clothes in a commercial fabric softener, she could sense the chemicals through smell and taste and because her bodily reaction was so strong she would not be able to be in the same room with them.

Obviously, the consequences of an exposure were very severe. For days after any exposure to chemicals or electromagnetic fields, she would feel like she had literally been run over by a truck. By now, social Annie was no longer fading, she was gone! She began to live her life in isolation and had very little contact with the outside world since even using a computer or talking on the phone was problematic. As you can imagine, this would be very difficult for anyone, but Annie wasn't anyone. Annie was someone who fed on social interaction. Suddenly, the only people she could be in contact with were those who were extremely environmentally aware and used only non-scented organic personal hygiene products. She could not visit her friends or family's homes as the obstacles were too huge and the risk of a severe reaction just too great. Due to this deliberating illness, Annie lost many of her friends and was even outcast by her church and her spiritual community. As you can well imagine, none of this helped with her depression. At times her will to live was very thin. Her lifeline to the everyday world you and I take for granted was getting thinner every day. As her symptoms continued to accelerate, she had to leave her partner, her home, her job, her friends, and in the process, she also lost her faith and her sense of herself. No longer able to work, or even participate in simple things in life like going to the dentist, the hairdresser, to a movie or merely hanging out with her friends, she felt like a total outcast. The only place where she felt okay was in nature. There, in that place where heaven and earth seem to come together, she reconnected to her faith and what sustains her.

This chemical sickness forced Annie to become focused solely on trying to find a cure that would allow her to have a fully functional life again. This led her to research and study into areas that might never have been of any particular interest if she had not suffered the consequences of MCS and EI.

Here's where the story starts to change direction and a small speck of light appears at the end of the tunnel. Annie's recovery started in July 2008 when she began using a series of psychological modalities that act on the brain to change brain structure and function (known as neuroplasticity). What this does is interrupt a brain trauma pattern; it resets normal limbic system function and inhibits the conditioned immune response. Through these psychological modalities, she was able to affect her neurology, which in turn changed her physiology. Annie experienced a huge shift within a three-day period and she continued to progressively get better over a period of about six months.

Annie's story, like that of anyone who has been through something traumatic and come out the other side, is heroic and courageous. And as is so often the case, at the time of the trauma we have no way of understanding that this event or set of circumstances is sculpting and refining both our character and our unique value set.

Let's go back to your unique value set. Before reading this you may never have even heard of Multiple Chemical Sensitivities or Electrical Sensitivities. If that's the case you probably don't know that there are literally tens of millions of people in the United States alone who are suffering the deliberating effects of these or related syndromes. Since you had no idea that chemical sickness exists, you would also have no idea how many people are suffering and looking for help on a daily basis. However, Annie, having gone through what I have just outlined, has now developed a unique value set that she can offer these people. The thing that seemed to threaten her very existence has become both the sustainer of and fulfiller of her existence.

As a Brain Retraining Specialist, Annie now assists others to overcome the same sickness that completely incapacitated her. Her focus is on acquired limbic system impairments and rehabilitation. She has gone on to develop a brain retraining workshop based on neuroplasticity called "The Dynamic Neural Retraining System" and is in the process of writing a book called "From Exile to Excellence: Healing Multiple Chemical Sensitivities through Neuroplasticity." She is now an international keynote speaker on Acquired Brain Injuries and Neuroplasticity.

By the way, I told you at the beginning that throughout this book I present many case studies of individuals. I did ask you to be aware that, for obvious reasons, the names and sometimes the gender of the person being referred to have been changed. However, Annie's name has not been changed as she has given me her permission to tell you her story in hopes of inspiring you not only to discovering your unique value set, but also to your greater health and awareness of something you may have previously had no knowledge of. If you want to find out more about Annie Hopper and the great work she does, go over to http://www.mcscure.com and take a look.

When that ego-mind of yours starts telling you that you have nothing to offer as a unique value set, tell it to "shut up" because, as I said earlier, if you've been on this planet for a while you have developed a unique value set, even if up until this very moment you weren't aware of it. When you own it, they will come and bang down your door to pay you for it.

You see each of us has our own unique value to offer even if it sometimes comes out of adversity, although that's certainly not the only way for you to discover your unique value set. Maybe you are a 55-year-old man or woman who is fascinated by model railways; maybe you have nursed an ailing partner, child or parent and you know what to do and you also know the emotional and mental weight of such a thing. Maybe you have a family recipe for chili, pie or some other stuff that everyone says is yummy. Maybe you speak "Klingon," or you know every swear word in Mandarin, Russian, Portuguese or ancient Egyptian. Maybe every child who knows you loves to hear your stories because when you tell them all the characters come to life. Maybe you know every variety of geranium and exactly how to take care of them. Maybe you know how to grow fresh tomatoes in the Northern hemisphere during the winter months. These are just a few ideas to get you started, but the truth is that you have unique value that you can offer the world.

At this point you may even have come up with something while your ego-mind is saying, "*Yeah, but lots of people can do that.*" Again, please remember, your ego-mind is a liar.

In case you don't believe me, let's just think about whether it's true that lots of people can do what you do. Let's say your unique value set is a dish you cook and your ego-mind wants to make it in to *no big deal, lots of people make this dish*. Is that true? Yes, of course there are all kinds of people cooking all kinds of dishes each and every day. Here's something worth considering. Have you ever been served your favorite food and when you got it you didn't like it? You knew there was something just not right about it? Or on another occasion, have you had your favorite dish and this time you were certain that this was the very best version of it you've ever eaten? Again the answer is yes, right? If it's your favorite food, how could you possibly like it from one place and dislike it from another? How can you like it one time and not the next? The answer is that your favorite food can be prepared and served in an infinite number of ways and each one is unique. Although there are thousands upon thousands of brilliant chefs, each one has a unique value in the way s/he prepares, cooks and serves that dish. When you find the one that pleases your palate the most, you will gladly pay them to make your favorite food.

In the same way, when you embrace your unique value, they will bang down your doors to give you money in exchange for the energy that is that unique value set, because even if someone else is doing it, they are not doing it the way you do.

All right, let's check in again. Is this making senses? Always remember, information without application has no value. That's why I ask you to stop and write about what you just learned throughout the book.

When you write down what you just learned, there is a greater likelihood of you taking it deeper into your subconscious mind, and as a result using the knowledge to change whatever's not working for you. As I keep saying, when you really get something, it goes deeper than it just making logical or rational sense. When you really "get it," you feel it. Something changes within you; more often than not, there is some visceral response. So, just check whether you are now having some other sensation of a shift, maybe that sudden silence in what had been a busy head, the gut reaction that tells you, *you're on to something here*. Make sure what you're reading is hitting home, and if you didn't have some kind of a "light bulb, ah hah moment" maybe it's worth going back and reading that last chapter again and looking for what your ego-mind may have dismissed that you need in order to become truly affluent.

Chapter 22

Why Helping Others Succeed Will Make You Rich

I know I keep repeating that discovering your unique value is about adding value to the world which in turn becomes a contribution that creates wealth not just for yourself but for all the people with whom you interact. However, I'm going to keep repeating it. Here's why: We have lived in extraordinarily competitive times, times that have bred greed and adversarial behaviors. It's clearly time to change this. As I've mentioned earlier in this book, times have changed, the economy has changed and we had better do the same even if your ego-mind is screaming at you to get or stay in a stable job. We must learn not be selfish about charging people for receiving what they get from you in the form of your Unique Value Set. To survive these new times, we all have got to change our approach to making money in the real world.

The approach I'm referring to throughout this book is one of cooperation and collaboration rather than competition. In another book I wrote called "*The 5 Foundations of Building Wealth From The Inside Out*,"

I shared that one of the foundations for building wealth from the inside out is the necessity of **Becoming Genuinely Relational**. Here's an excerpt from that book so you can see how tapping into your unique value can create wealth, not only for you but also with and for others.

We have lived in a highly competitive time and many approach business (and each other) from a very Darwinian stance of dog-eat-dog. The result of this kind of approach is that when it comes to sales, you may be able to undercut your competition, but you will never build a loyal customer following because the people you are chasing are only chasing a better deal. When the better deal/cheaper price arrives, they will dump you like a hot potato. All too often in the dog-eat-dog approach, your customer or potential customer can feel like they are nothing more than the prey you are hunting.

Becoming genuinely relational means you must stop being "a hunter." A hunter is a person who sees other people as objects that exist purely to help s/he get where s/he wants to go. That is the antithesis of becoming genuinely relational. Becoming genuinely relational means that when you meet people, you do so with only one question on your mind, "How can I help this person succeed?" You avoid the hunter approach which asks, "What can this person do to help me?"

Please write that down. "How can I help this person succeed?" Now, even though you may think you understand what I'm talking about here, even though you may have been long aware of the concept, please write it down anyway because when we get complacent about <u>what we think we know</u>, we risk losing it altogether.

When we ask the question "How can I help this person succeed?", we are approaching them and living from a place of being in the flow of affluence rather than from a place of lack mentality which believes there's not enough, and as a result such a person acts, or rather re-acts, as if they have got to grab anything and everything that passes by. The genuinely relational approach is totally different in that we are not talking about helping someone succeed by selling him or her our product, even though they may end up buying our product or service, that's not on our agenda. No, we are talking about how *you, as a person*, can help the other person succeed or have more success than they are already having even if it has nothing to do with what you offer.

One of the things that causes business downturns is hoarding. Hoarding in any of its forms—and that includes becoming an infor-mation hoarder—is a sign of lack mentality and will not bring you the kind of success you are looking for. (That's one of the reasons I ask you to think about with whom you can share what you are learning.) There are, of course, all kinds of information hoarding. However, the one I want to address here is the type of hoarding in which someone gathers copious amounts of information about themselves, their company, and their products. Now you may be wondering why someone would do this beyond the obvious product knowledge etc. Well, the drive behind this kind of behavior is so that this might become or at least appear "interesting," and makes their company and their product more interesting.

Now here's where we veer away from lack thinking into a more abundant mindset. A genuinely relational person is <u>not</u> about being interesting—she or he is all about being *interested*.

Please write that down; it is very important.

**Become focused on being genuinely interested
rather than interesting.**

The fact that every great salesperson knows and so few sales people apply is that people do not buy products and services from interesting people. They buy products and services from friends. Why? Because they like friends, they trust friends and friends are *interested in them*. When you become genuinely relational, you are like a good friend, and good friends care about the people they are interacting with and are genuinely interested in them.

Approaching not just business but life from the place of being genuinely relational with others is not only vital to your mental, emotional, spiritual, and financial growth and development, it largely determines how much you can and will enjoy your life.

Those who do not become genuinely relational lose so much because without having loving, caring, giving relationships with others, we are not only being robbed of one of life's greatest pleasures, but we're also robbing others of the amazing benefits, gifts and growth they would enjoy by engaging with us. Here's the truth of it, no one ever truly knows the difference we've made or the impact we have on the world. Nonetheless, you can be certain that you have made a difference, that you have had an impact, and I think you'd agree that it's the kind of impact that counts. Therefore may I suggest that each day we all need to become a little more committed to being genuinely relational. Because we benefit every bit as much as those we relate with.

So once more, write it down. If you want to become more successful **Become interested, rather than interesting.**

Just take a moment, don't even bother reading on for a moment or two. Just let it really sink in how important relationships are to you getting, growing, and keeping wealth. Then take it a step deeper. You want more dough, right? Well, who has the money that you want? I don't mean specifically as in "Fred Brown" or "Susan Green." When you let this soak in, you realize that the money you are looking for is with people, right? So doesn't it make logical sense to cultivate your relationships? To put this in the simplest form possible: The more people you know, the easier it is to make loads of money. You need to become committed to being of service because, and this is the tricky part, people buy from people they like and trust so the service you are providing must be given genuinely in order to be of service.

Is this making senses? Can you really let it in? It's not about going to every networking meeting within a thirty-mile radius in order to meet more people. Why? Because they will forget you just as quickly as they met you if they don't feel that you are authentically interested in them.

Actually, if you really want to get this at a cellular level all you have to do is remember a time when you met someone who was all hand-shakes and smiles, saying all the right things, and you just got the feeling that you were being slimed. That, my friend, is someone who is <u>not</u> genuinely relational, and I know that you can feel that you never want to come across like that, do you?

Chapter 23

Your Dad's Job is Gone

Many of the people in our parents' generation grew up with and passed on a message that said we should find a good solid job, climb our way through the ranks and eventually we'll be all right. The "climb your way through the ranks" part is where things became "success at any cost" for many people. This of course makes no room for being genuinely relational. The fact is that many of those companies whose ranks you might have tried to climb through are gone. Many Blue Chip companies have become fiscal dinosaurs that cannot sustain themselves let alone those who attached themselves to it as a means of security. Our parents' generation in the corporate sun is done. Those who enter the traditional workforce are now faced with many of the challenges that were more traditionally faced by entrepreneurial types. In today's job market, you have got to be willing to not only think, but go outside the box, do more, and do better than the parameters of what your job description suggests. Above all, to make it in the business world these days, you better be sincerely interested. Interested in your company, their products and most of all the people you service. Outsourcing customer service to foreign countries has happened because the successful companies know that if they are to find, keep, and grow their place in the marketplace they better take care of their customer. Sadly, this falls through the cracks if the customer gets through to an agent who doesn't speak the language necessary to provide that customer care. In fact, the companies who are at the top of the curve are the ones who do not just answer customer service questions. No, the top companies are all about creating relationships and to do that you must be "interested and flexible." It is that flexibility that will make the difference between those who sink and those who fly.

In the early 90s, top companies were surveyed and one of the questions they were asked was whether they would hire someone who had changed careers twice or more. The overwhelming response was clear and unmistakable: "No!" Further research showed that these companies viewed such a person as *professionally unstable*.

In the first years of the new millennium the top companies were once again asked the same question, only this time they were asked whether they would hire someone who had changed careers not twice but three or more times. Once again there was an overwhelmingly clear response, only this time it was "Yes." When asked why they would hire such a person, the replies indicated that the companies view such a person *as being flexible and in times such as these, being adaptable to changes in technology and the market place is an asset.*

That's a good thing because the latest research from the US Department of Labor says that today's learner will have ten to fourteen jobs by the age of 38. The reality is that your dad's jobs are gone. If they haven't been replaced by technology, they've been outsourced. The ones that are left are with companies that had previously been considered unshakable, but today are looking for government assistance just to stay afloat.

This means we must look at wealth building as something more than that great job with the amazing company who will fly you all over the world and pick you up in limos. That's a fantasy of a bygone era. So, again it comes down to building relationships and having the flexibility to shift and change with whatever comes around the next corner.

Does that make senses? Such a person can bring more to the table. Relationship building skills and flexibility are key.

In all my years of research, there is one thing I know for sure—wealthy people do not have all their eggs in one basket. Even though the wealthy have usually picked a specific focus for their business (which is often something they really get a lot of joy from), they do not rely upon that one thing to keep their cash flowing. The truly wealthy understand that in order to create, maintain, and grow wealth you must have multiple streams of income and some of those streams need to be passive and residual.

Later I'll go into more detail as to what "Passive" and "Residual" means in the context of wealth, but for now just understand that it means you don't have to put hours upon hours, day upon days, weeks up on weeks or years upon years into something in order to have it continue to bring you income. Having passive-residual income means that you do something to generate an income once and then it flows to you repeatedly with minimum effort on your part. But before we take a look at how to develop passive-residual income, we need to understand why so many very bright people keep working in jobs they don't particularly like and that, in all likelihood, are ill fitted to their natural talent and the unique value they have to offer.

So let's see, this was a short and punchy chapter and as usual I want to be sure it's making senses to you? Are you really getting it that if you've changed careers more than once that's an asset in today's market? The change in the economy has been devastating to many, and I in no way want to minimize the devastating effect that has had on many individuals and families. However, that being said, the change in the economy has been enormously freeing for many people who would not have had the testicles (or ovaries) to leave a job they either hated or were bored out of their mind at if they hadn't have been laid off. I sincerely believe that ten years after the great depression of 2009 people will look back and realize what a gift that crash ultimately brought.

In my opinion, there are still far too many people getting up every morning to go to work in jobs that drain their souls. It's sad to me that so many people gave up their dreams in pursuit of steady hours, more "stuff" and a pension at the end. Unfortunately when the bomb dropped on the economy, those folks had no shelter to hide in.

Recognizing that your unique value set has come out of all your experiences, including the ones that sucked the big hotdog when they were happening, gives you flexibility, freedom from feeling like a victim and ultimately the ability to captain your own ship of dreams. If I may, let me challenge you to really feel the truth of that.

Chapter 24

The Ph.D. Sized Lie about How to Get Rich

The concept of passive-residual income can be a major paradigm shift for those of us who grew up with the traditional corporate definition of success. Very few of us escaped the message that was drummed in at every turn, "Go to school and get good grades, so that you can go to college and can get a good job." Of course getting the good job was just the first step on the corporate ladder. Once you got the job, you must work hard and then you'll be promoted, so you can buy a nice car, nice house, and contribute to a retirement plan. That way at 65 you can enjoy your "Golden Years."

Well, just in case no one noticed, the global economy has changed and more people over the age of 60 are in the work force today than at any other time in history. There are 77 million baby boomers—a quarter of the US population—who will be reaching the traditional retirement age by 2012. Many of these boomers aren't ready to retire because they still feel, and it's likely very true, that they still have lots to contribute. Other boomers simply can't retire because they would be without an income. According to researchers at Rutgers University, "The traditional notion of retirement is obsolete."

One of the reasons retirement is obsolete and "your dad's job is gone" is because of what I call "corporate hypnosis," a concept many people have bought into part and parcel. At the front end of that corporate hypnosis is that push to get a post-secondary education. I'm not, in any way, saying you shouldn't go to college and I'm certainly not implying that if you did, you made a mistake. What I am saying is that college degrees are not actually a prerequisite for most careers and getting one isn't really necessary for most people. Stay with me here and you'll see exactly what I mean.

Don't you think it's a little crazy that you're supposed to choose something to study as a means of taking you in the direction of what you plan on doing once you are out of college/university. Furthermore, you were supposed to do this straight out of high school when most people can't even decide on what to wear from one day to the next. The fact is that most people who are in their fifties still don't know what they want to be when they grow up, and trying to decide that at eighteen—well it's a stretch to say the least.

Now maybe you went to college/university and maybe you didn't, nevertheless in my experience the large majority of people entering colleges haven't got the faintest idea what they want to do after they graduate. The ones that think they know very often do one of two things—change their mind half way through or stick with it just because that's what they chose and they don't want to look foolish. I know that doesn't happen to everyone, but I'd put money on it being a large majority of them. (This is the reason "mature students" do so much better in college and university. They are older, have been out in the world and even if they haven't found their life's passion, they are absolutely certain, via experience, what they don't want to do or be. So, when they choose to study something, it's because they really want to study it.)

To be blunt; if you want to pursue a life of true economic and time freedom, college/university doesn't seem to offer what you really need. As I said, I'm not knocking a post secondary education. I just want us to look at it outside of the corporate hypnosis. There are many advantages to the process. College and university assist many people in getting out from under the parental apron strings, obtain a better sense of their own identity, see things in a bigger context, and frankly for many, explore their sexuality. In addition, the years at college are often ones of learning how to learn, which is a very valuable skill set, not to mention, some careers absolutely require post-secondary education. If your dream is to be a brain surgeon or argue cases before the Supreme Court, you will need to go to college or university, no question. However, for most people who are on the path to financial freedom, college and university will unlikely provide you with the kind of specialized knowledge necessary to become anything that resembles wealthy.

Napoleon Hill in the classic "Think and Grow Rich" book said, "There are two kinds of knowledge. One is general, the other is specialized. General knowledge, no matter how great in quantity or variety it may be, is of but little use in the accumulation of money."

Let's be honest, our moms, dads, and the whole of secondary education have done a fabulous job of selling the idea that perpetuates the corporate hypnosis that claims college grads have the best chance in the job market. (Admittedly, that part is most likely true to some extent.) Once in the job market and employed by the big company, college grads can then look forward to spending the next 10, 15, 25 years climbing the increasingly steep corporate ladder. However, the fun is not over yet. Just because you want to climb the ladder doesn't mean you will be allowed to do it at your pace. (Particularly if you are a woman or a minority.)

Oh no, the ONLY way you can increase your income and climb that ladder is by making sure that the right people are seeing you slogging away, and if you are "lucky" they will "give" you your promotion.

Small segue here: In many ways I see this as why so many first world countries are in trouble: The work force has realized that it's very important to be "seen as busy" (you want the promotion, so you've got to look busy), but busy and productive can be vastly different things. Busy is often a drain on the company coffers. People paid by the hour will fill the hour with something, even if it's not productive, right? Truth be told, many people are in the business of busy-ness.

Many individuals have been sold on the certainty that a college degree is the only way to earn a respectable salary. Nevertheless, it's worth asking why there are an ever-increasing number of highly educated people who are unemployed and struggling to make ends meet? I agree that there was a time when a degree would give you a big leg up, but as far as I can see, that world is gone. The result is that people with bachelor's degrees are working in appliance stores as salespeople and customer service.

By the way, you know who this corporate hypnosis works for besides the corporations? Colleges and universities, that's who! Why? Because as more and more people are pouring extra tens of thousands of dollars into taking their education to the next level, a simple college degree has lost most of its value in the competitive market place, and so people believe that further investment in their academic career will make all the difference. The colleges and universities are quite happy to take their money to give them that degree they think they need to succeed.

Globally, each and every year, hundreds of thousands of young adults buy this corporate hypnosis. They study hard and aspire to participate by investing in the business of education where they pay to be the product. And what a glorious multi-billion dollar business it is. In the US today the average college entrant spends around $100,000 and four years of his or her life to get a degree. At the end of those four years that individual will receive an official piece of paper at an event where they can celebrate the conclusion of cramming for exams, spending around a hundred grand and possibly doing many things that they won't want talked about in a future business meeting by throwing their hats in the air. Then they get to go out in the world and compete for a job against all the other people who did exactly the same thing. They've invested all that time and all that money and in return they get the honor of competing for a job that will, in all likelihood, pay around $30,000 to $40,000 as a return on their investment of around $100,000. There's an acronym for this that I've mentioned a couple of times already and it seems very appropriate to say it again—JOB= **J**ust **O**ver **B**roke.

Let me give you a real-life example of what I'm talking about.

> Loraine had been a pretty good student during high school. She didn't get into any major problems and was very good at looking good even when she was being bad. She had been on the honor roll in grade ten. However, in grades eleven and twelve even though she had decided to go to college, she just didn't work that hard. She didn't need to. She realized something that most of her fellow students hadn't; beyond a certain grade average, there was no point in pushing because it didn't make much difference to the university she wanted to attend. Using her great memory, she could work just hard enough to qualify for a scholarship.

When Loraine got to the University it was all very exciting. The campus was both beautiful and huge. There were all kinds of things to explore; classes she was fascinated by and even ones she could drop in on, and there were new and wise profs to advise her. There were lots of very cute guys on campus and great bars in which to meet them. She felt like a kid in a sexually charged, academic candy store. The first few weeks were a little disorienting, trying to find classes and working with a schedule that was very different than that of high school, yet it was all still very exciting. The first semester flew by. Exam time came and Loraine was shocked to discover that it wasn't going to be the kind of breeze that high school had been. Her memory was not going to get her through and when she received her first C-, she was devastated.

By the time Loraine was at the end of her third year and about to embark on the final year of study and her resulting degree, she had considered changing majors three separate times and to three different subjects. Even though Loraine had seriously doubted whether she had finally chosen the right subject to study, she was committed to completing, to getting that important piece of paper in her hands. In her final year, Loraine buried herself in her studies, telling herself that this was the key to a better job and a better life, and she was not going to waste all the money she now owed in student loans.

After graduation with a BA under her belt, Loraine went out into the work force. It was 1995 and she was certain that the future was bright. Loraine had looked around for the "right" job but hadn't found a fit, so she decided that she would just take an average job in order to not fall behind on her student loans. Besides which, she desperately wanted to move out of her parents' house. It didn't take long before she found herself working as a sales person in a big box electronics store. Within a couple of months she was bored, frustrated and seriously considering applying to go back to school to get a Masters degree in the same subject she had done her BA in. She made some inquires, and within a short period of time, she had pretty much made up her mind about what she would do. However, that was going to be at least another nine months away.

A few weeks later, while Loraine was working on the floor of the store, she received a call from head office asking her to come in and interview for an assistant buyer's position. Even though she was sure the company was not where she wanted to be in five years or even nine months, she thought that maybe her four years of university was beginning to show some dividends.

The following week she was well dressed and maybe a little over confident as she walked into the interview. She nailed it! The following Monday morning she was out of the store uniform and at the head office dressed like a young executive. The job was stressful and invigorating; she was being challenged to think outside the box. The company was relatively young;

they had opened up in an exploding market and they were growing in leaps and bounds. Within six months, she had been promoted again and was loving the fact that she was traveling quite a lot as the company opened more and more stores.

One night in a hotel room, she was on the phone with her sister who asked her something that she had thrown to the back of her mind every time it had snuck up. This time the question was coming from outside, her sister, and Loraine felt confronted when she asked, "Have you applied to grad school yet?" It was an innocent enough question asked without any agenda. However, Loraine's reply was short, sharp, and brimming with the need to prove she was doing the right thing.

"Look it's no one's business whether I go back to school or not. I'm going to do what's right for me?"

Needless to say, the conversation frittered out fairly quickly and as a result of her harshness with her sister, Loraine had a hard time sleeping. The next morning she looked tired, so she took extra care with her make-up as she went to meet the head of sales for this region. She decided to think about her decision later at which point she would call her sister and apologize.

Loraine walked in to the big downtown head office building and as she did, she went into business mode. Pressing the button in the crowded elevator, she had an intuition that something was up. However, she wasn't sure if it was good or bad. Exiting the elevator, her eyes were drawn to the giant company logo and it hit her, this was the big place. This was command central.

As Loraine reentered the elevator after her meeting, she was doing her best to hold in her excitement. She was already thinking about where she would live, the new clothes she'd need and all the amazing opportunities that she had been told were before her. She was totally pleased with herself for having risen through the ranks so quickly. She rushed back to the hotel to call her sister and tell her the good news before anyone else. "I got it. I got the job," she said almost screaming with excitement.

Her sister was having trouble even understanding Loraine as she continued telling her that she had no idea that they intended to offer her a position. What Loraine's sister did catch was that she would be moving to Toronto, a city that was more than two thousand miles away. Her sister suddenly felt mixed emotions. She was excited for Loraine's career advancement, yet she was disappointed that there would be such distance between them. She also was quietly concerned for Loraine. You see Loraine's degree was in textile arts and it was obvious that this career move would mean that she would be leaving even further behind something that she always loved.

Within three years Loraine was married to a good guy, Alan. She had met him at a company function; he was a friend of a coworker. They had felt a quick connection and were married within a year of meeting. Alan wanted kids, so did Loraine—but not just yet. Loraine was still putting in about 65 hours a week and although the money was great, she was not yet where she wanted to be in the company.

As the months went by, Alan and Loraine were fighting more and more. They were both tired and overworked because they were both struggling to climb their respective corporate ladders and for some reason unknown to either of them, each was stalled.

It was a particularly cold Tuesday morning when Loraine got a call from a headhunter who wanted to meet with her for lunch that day. The headhunter offered Loraine just what she wanted and a little more than she had hoped for in the money department. There was only one glitch; she would have to move again. And, of course, there would be added responsibility, which in turn would mean more hours for a while as well.

It was a hard decision, but within three months Loraine was living in Chicago. She and Alan had decided they were going to see how they could work out a long distance relationship, but Loraine knew it was just a matter of time.

Over the next few months, she was incredibly busy and often wondered what would have happened if she hadn't taken a job at the electronics store selling computers and CDs with all the other people who also seemed to have a BA degree in something or other. She wondered what would have happened if she'd have gone back and got her Master's degree. She, of course, wondered what would have happened to her and Alan if she hadn't have gotten this great job in Chicago. But the thing that she wondered the most about was whether she has what it takes to be out in the world, not working for or dependant on a company for a pay cheque? You see, every morning as Loraine was on her way to work she would drive through the "artsy" area of town. This was the same area that, when she was in town on weekends, she would walk through and fantasize about having a little store there where she would sell imported fabrics and baubles from around the world. You see Loraine had always dreamed of designing and developing exotic fabric. It was the reason she had been attracted to studying textile arts when she first went to college, even though she had ended up with a "more practical" business degree.

Loraine could sometimes find a little compensation when she looked around her apartment decorated with beautiful fabrics from around the world. Loraine already had lots of friends here in Chicago all of whom really liked and admired her for her accomplishments and her taste. Sometimes her sister would ask her about her dream and Loraine, having now been trained in corporate negotiations, had become very skilful at changing the subject. However, that didn't make it go away...

As we can learn from Loraine's journey, all kinds of diversions can distract us on the way to our dreams. There's a trap in thinking that because we're smart we don't need to work so hard. It is easier to justify losing track of your dreams in a tidal wave of wonderful distractions disguised as promises laid out like crumbs in a fairy tale taking us to a higher level of status and often a deeper abandonment of our soul's path. These crumbs can be things like a better office, more pay, and a myriad of other shiny prizes. Yes, if we measure success by climbing the corporate ladder, it's clear that Loraine was successful. However, on the odd occasion when you could catch her off guard, talking about fabric, its weave and its design, when you would see the lights come on in her eyes, you might question how she or, for that matter, any of us measure our success.

The harsh truth is that school, whether secondary or post secondary, does NOT teach you much about how to actually be in the world or how to make money. It does however indirectly offer to teach you how, if you so choose, to sell a piece of your soul so that people will like you and it teaches you how to stay DEPENDENT on a system that is at this point in history going down the pipe faster than yesterday's lunch.

Much of what we learn in college sets us up to follow the rules of participating in the high stress, hamster wheel called the corporate world. And let's face it, with school fees being what they are, many very good students leave college or university with a high GPA and a very low credit score having destroyed their credit rating by not being able to pay back the loans they took out to get an education in order to get a good job in hopes of making big money.

Again I feel it's very important for me to reiterate that if, in fact, you are a part of corporate America or any other corporate culture and you absolutely love what you do and you get out of bed each and every day with a spring in your step, I am delighted for you and I want you to know I was not and am not speaking to you.

However, if you are someone who feels like that hamster, stay with me…

I realize that some of you reading this are somewhere up that ladder. There seems to be no way off and I want you to know that's not true. Then again, if you fully bought into the corporate hypnosis and it's not really your dream, for as long as you go along with it, you're stuck. You will have to do what they tell you—and then some—until someone higher up, someone that you may never have even met, decides to let you have another rung on the ladder and with it will likely come with more money and just as likely a lot more work and stress. When you think that's what most people do to "guarantee" a good income, it's more than a bit loony, isn't it?

Listen, even with everything I'm saying here, I am in no way judging you for doing what you've done. My belief is that you likely did the best you could with what you knew, but, at the same time, it's important to know that what you knew was spoon-fed to you by a system that I have no evidence of having your best interest at heart. The bottom line is that, as far as we know, you only get to live this life once, and to live it letting someone else, (or something else) dictate how you're going to live is rather sad. I believe you deserve better than corporate slavery.

At this point you may be thinking (and I wouldn't be surprised if you were) that I'm opposed to all post secondary education and climbing the corporate ladder. If that's what you're thinking, I would like to make it very clear that I'm neither for nor against either of those things. If, having truly considered that college and the corporate ladder are what you want, and you've decided that this is the path to not only your financial success but also to your greatest joy, I couldn't be happier for you.

However, if someone(s) is pressuring you to go to college, and you are weighing the pros and cons you might want to consider this: Take a look at whether a degree or degrees is actually what you need in order to do what you truly want to do. It's simple when you think about it. If you absolutely love tinkering with cars, fixing pipes, or growing plants, then you don't really need an academic degree as much as you need specific training. You may be able to get that training through an apprenticeship program, a specialized course, or a technical school. However, if what you want is to be able to design and build cars, create a new type of plumbing system, or delve into the genetics of plant science, you may want to consider more education. Staying with this, if you are absolutely on fire with the idea of becoming a lawyer, a doctor, a surgeon, or such, the system, whether you like it or not, needs you to have a higher level of post secondary education. If you flip it around you'll definitely understand why. You wouldn't want to be wheeled into the operating theater for major surgery and be greeted by someone who says, "I don't have a lot of training in this, but I read a couple of books and I really think I'll have a flair for it" would you? No, I think not, not any more than you would want to be brought in to court on false charges and discover that the person who is defending you just doesn't happen to have the level of post secondary education, including a degree in law that you'll need in order to stay out of jail.

Seriously, put some thought into this. Some career paths absolutely require university degrees, and some don't. Your job is to discern the difference rather than behaving automatically. That way you will know when you are following your own path rather than indoctrinated rhetoric. For instance, did you know that the top ten in-demand jobs in 2010 did not exist in 2004? Students studying a four-year technical degree today will discover that half of what they learn in their first year will be completely outdated by the time they are in their third year of that degree program. That's because the amount of technical information is doubling every two years. Today, as you read this, one in four workers has been with their current employer less than a year. Once again we see that the idea of becoming a company man or woman for the next twenty-five years is becoming the ghost of a time gone by.

If the economy has changed in any kind of a permanent way, which it appears it has, then looking for solutions the way we used to just doesn't make sense. We must be willing to question what we presuppose as the truth. It doesn't matter whether that's about our religious beliefs, our ability to take responsibility for our health, or our ability to become financially abundant.

I'm not a pessimist about our economy. I am, however, an optimistic realist. I realize that some may see this as idealistic, but I'm someone who believes that an economy run by a work force of people doing what they love will not only create greater and greater levels of healthy financial abundance, but also greater levels of emotional and spiritual health and stability.

In the traditional model of success, you're hypnotized into believing the false promise that if you work really hard, give up time with the people you love and trade the best years of your life, you'll be able to retire at age 65. That means after about 40 or so years of nonsense, you will finally have the time and financial means to go on those trips you dreamed of and do some nice things for your grandchildren. What this is really saying is that you get to work your ass off for many decades until the system has used you up and you're too old, drained, and frail to have fun and actually enjoy the time off. What's even sadder is that the old model isn't working anymore; retirement plans are down the toilet and the average person is dead within seven years of retiring. Like I said, when you think about it, it's nuttier that your aunt Aggie's Christmas fruit cake, right?

So what's the option?

Maybe real success is measured in passion for doing what you love. Maybe real success is when you speak of your work, you do it with a fire in your belly and a light in your eyes. And maybe real success is while all this is going on, you still have time for a life outside of your work.

Make senses? Look, my friend, I don't for a second expect you to agree with every word I say. However, I do want you to at least be open-minded enough to do your best to objectively evaluate what I'm sharing with you, even if it rubs you the wrong way. I'm not here to put anyone down, and if you've got this far in the book, you know that, right? A few chapters back, I explained to you that one of the reasons I was compelled to put in the research, time, energy, and effort to write this book was because I have a desire to assist people in becoming free. If that means challenging some of the ideas you've held as sacred, I'm willing to go there. Why? Because I care, and the people who care are willing to show you the truth, because sometimes The Truth Hurts Before It Sets You Free!

Chapter 25

There's Nothing Passive about Residual Income

I'm going to take a chance and say that somewhere along the line you've already worked out that it's time to get off the hamster wheel or else you wouldn't have picked up this book. Well, a wonderful way to do that is to create something that produces passive-residual income. Sounds like a dream? Seems impossible? If it does, it's because you have been operating under that corporate hypnosis.

Passive-residual income is a way to create wealth and find greater levels of freedom while still paying your bills along the way. Many great books have been written on the subject so I'm not going to take pages up writing lists, but what I will tell you is grab a hold of what I believe is one of the best books on the subject of how to free yourself from that wheel: Tim Ferriss's "The 4-Hour Work Week." It's well written and absolutely full of great resources for you to be able to live well by working only four hours a week, (well, if not 4 hours a week, then at least a lot less than you've been working).

To make things as simple as possible, just know that passive income means you make money without a direct or continuous effort. Do you like the sound of that? You can search the term and you'll discover literally millions of web pages offering ways to make passive-residual income. (Before you ask, I cannot personally recommend any one in particular, but I do suggest you do your own due diligent research.)

For now, perhaps the best way to illustrate the wealth potential of passive income is with a man by the name of Ray Crock. Ray was the founder of the McDonald's™ franchise. Although most people in the world know the name McDonald's™, surprisingly few know its founder's name. But Ray was a master of passive income and he can teach us a thing or two about how and why it works.

But first, ask yourself if you think that Ray Crock went down to every burger shop and started flipping burgers whenever he wanted to get paid? No, of course he didn't. He set up a system for earning money passively, and you can too. It may not be through a burger franchise, but I guarantee there is a way for you, if you are willing to look and take action.

Franchising is not the only way to build passive income. Many other forms can work equally well depending on what lights your fire. Investing in real estate is one that stands out although, as I'm sure you are aware, success in that venue depends on the contemporary market and your level of knowledge and skills in that market. That being said the people who will be making the big bucks in a crashed housing market are the people buying properties for pennies on the dollar. Let's face it, history shows that the housing market will return, and when it does those people who bought in the down time will be the ones laughing while others are crying about how they "should have" back then.

The second way to build wealth on a part-time basis is through residual income. Residual income means money that flows to you on a regular basis whether you are in the office or on a holiday. Often it's like someone paying rent on your concept, idea, or invention.

As I said, I cannot recommend one particular form of passive or residual income if only because that is not the purpose of this book. What I will share with you here is that I know you will find massive value in the techniques and understanding that have made every millionaire on this planet successful.

But first we need to collapse one more of those money myths we've been talking about. Despite what you're heard...

Time Is Not Money!

In all the years I've invested in the study of, and research on what it takes to achieve lasting success, I've come to understand and believe in something deeply because I've seen it at work time and time again in the lives of millionaires and billionaires the world over. What millionaires and billionaires truly understand is this:

Trading your time for money is never going to make you wealthy.

Do you really understand what that means? Look, I know you were told that if you accumulate enough credentials you would be making the big bucks. You were told this because part of the hypnosis is that with each credential comes an increase in the hourly rate you earn or can charge. That part is somewhat true—get more credentials in a specific area and your hourly rate will go up. But a better set of questions to consider are: What's the maximum you can make in any given hour? Will that ever be enough? And, what if there was a way to multiply that hourly rate?

Here's the news flash. No one ever became massively wealthy by trading time for money. No matter what job you're in, every single person who is selling his or her time for money is going to face the same limiting challenge.

The number of hours in a day is limited and the amount of money you can charge for each one of those hours is also limited. For instance; a top-level corporate financial consultant working for one of the biggest financial companies at this time earns between $250–$300 an hour; an orthodontist brings in around $200–$250 per hour. Top lawyers make $1,000 an hour. A brain surgeon commands a top dollar, but even a brain surgeon is never going to become immensely wealthy just by doing brain surgery, no matter how good they are or how many operations they squeeze into a day.

What it comes down to is that in order to develop wealth consciousness, to be in the flow of affluence, in order to create real wealth, you must get past the need to have someone else guarantee your income. I know that even the thought of leaving a regular, steady paying job can be very scary for some folks. However, if you are living your life from a place of being absolutely reliant on someone else for your financial flow, then you are not yet living in a place of wealth consciousness! Next news headline: To get out of this cycle, you must be willing to start some kind of business of your own.

What's that? You're scared? You don't want to quit your job? You've got bills to pay and mouths to feed; you depend on the steady job for your health insurance plan, and after all, that orthodontist is charging $200 an hour.

Who said anything about quitting your job? Many of the most successful people began building a business on a part-time basis. There are a couple of ways you can do this that are proven to work. One is residual income and the other is passive income. Either one is good, but both are better.

If you grew up with the "time is money" mantra, then what you are doing is leveraging your time for an hourly rate, e.g. one hour of your time spent in production for XYZ Company pays you X number of dollars. That's time leveraged for money.

Is this making Senses? Just sit for a moment and let yourself think back over what you've read in this last chapter. Consider what it was that gave you your light bulb moments? What rang your bells, or sent shivers down your spine? What was that moment when you "got it?" Was it when you saw the words on the page and they seemed to suddenly slow down and echo in your head? Was it when you realized that you had been trading your time for money and it was never going to make you wealthy?

Whatever it was that created your moment of awakening, great! Take it in, write about it in your journal and share it with a friend. Just let yourself feel it in whatever way works for you so that you can begin to now apply the subconscious tactics of the truly affluent and put the power of leverage on your side.

So, how can you do that? How can you start putting the power of leverage on your side? As you might guess, that's what we are going to talk about next.

Chapter 26

The Power of Leverage

"The first rule of any technology used in a business is that automation applied to an efficient operation will magnify the efficiency."

~*Bill Gates*

One of the ways wealthy people are different from the regular struggling individual is that they use leverage in order to create wealth. This is, in fact, one of their (and it can be your) great competitive edges. However, they are not leveraging themselves for a higher hourly rate. That's not their model. They create passive income by using leverage in ways most people would never even consider. Those who are wealthy leverage their own time and other people's time; they leverage technology, and yes, they even know how to leverage money. This takes them away from being dependant and in turn multiplies their earning power so they can produce not just passive income, but very often multiple streams of it.

Anyone of us who have even seen a Wile E. Coyote cartoon knows what a physical lever is. Most of us grew up watching Wile E. use one in his fruitless attempts at catching the Road Runner. However, in reality, levers are simple powerful tools that go back to the beginning of civilized man. In mechanical terms, a lever is any instrument that allows us to magnify an applied force to have a greater impact. However, there are far more uses for a lever than getting boulders out of the way. Leverage can be an extraordinarily powerful tool for those people who don't have too much to invest. But you don't have to take my word for it...

Leveraging Money

Many years ago I met Robert Allen, the author of many books including "Multiple Streams of Internet Income" (In fact my name and input is on page 246 of that book). Robert is famous for teaching people how to leverage their money via real estate. According to him, it doesn't matter what shape the market is in; you just leverage in accordance with the market because the way you leverage money is by borrowing money to buy an income-producing asset that will in turn produce more money than the loan you have against it. In his real estate course, he shows how it's possible to buy a $100,000 house with only a 5 percent or $5,000 down payment. What that means is that this person now potentially has control of a $100,000 asset with only a $5,000 down payment

But before you go any further, I don't want you to think that I somehow missed the news. At the time I'm writing this, the housing market is in the gutter. Again, the one thing that history teaches us is that it will not stay that way. I know that many people got burned on bad deals. But know this, the people who lost everything when the real estate bubble burst were not people who were leveraging. They were people who were gambling. Buying a home on an interest-only loan with the hopes that you'll make 20 or 30 grand over the next three to six months is more of a gamble than taking your paycheck down to the casino and putting it all on the roll of the dice because you heard there has been a lot of winners down there this week.

Despite what you've been fed via a hysterical media if, even in a crappy market, a $100,000 house appreciates by a modest 5 percent per year that will equate to a 100 percent return on your $5,000 investment. In the US today the interest rate on a savings account is less than 1 percent, so there's not a bank out there that is willing to pay that kind of interest you would make on that real estate.

I'm not here to pass judgment on those who got into the real estate market during the bubble. Many of the people I know and love were involved. They, like so many others, saw the situation as a way out of whatever financial challenges they were having. Many people genuinely thought they were leveraging, when what they were doing was looking for a magic bullet or something that would instantly solve all their problems. Sadly, many of these folks overextended themselves and went bankrupt. So while I'm not here to judge; I am going to caution you—please do not confuse leveraging with gambling or some sort of magical solution. Financial leveraging is a strategy, and as with all strategies, it must be learned and, at least at the beginning, fairly rigidly practiced. As far as I'm concerned, this is the area of leveraging where I would highly suggest you get help from an expert. In fact, my best advice on this is simple—get direction from a couple of different experts who have expertise in different areas of the same thing. It never hurts to have a second, or third, opinion. After all, Bernie Madoff was an expert who defrauded thousands of investors out of billions of dollars and I'm guessing you know what happened to the people who didn't get a second opinion.

Leveraging Technology

Things change, we all know that. Sometimes we like those changes, sometimes we don't, but change is unavoidable. Deal with it!

Some of those changes, when they first come about, particularly when it comes to technology can be a little frustrating. The learning curve never seems to ease up. You, me, all of us these days are living in a science fiction future and taking much of it for granted. Take a random example—cell phones. Some of us are old enough to remember a time where there were no cell phones. Then somewhat magically the day came when you saw someone (probably in a movie) in their car or walking down the street chatting away on their brick. That's quite literally what people called them because these things weighed a ton and were the size of a house brick. Nowadays, who doesn't have a cell phone? Is your cell simply for emergency use? Or has it become something you'd feel lost without? Cell phones now are major contributors to daily life. You can use them to take pictures, even videos of your friends, family and even news events. Most people's cell phones play music, browse the web and some with the right app will even make fart sounds for you—if that's what you want.

Everything is changing. Only one hundred years ago, the life expectancy of a man was 49 and 53 for a woman. Today life expectancy for a man is 65 and 69 for a woman. In some countries, like Japan, men can expect to live to 79 and women to 86. We are living in a science fiction future of filmless cameras and magic pills that grow hair on bald heads. Men in their 80's are fathering children and women in their 50's are birthing them.

The fact of the matter is that you can try to fight progress, telling yourself and everyone else why it sucks, but whining and moaning will not make it go away. As I'm sure you're aware, humans have been around for a while and fighting against progress seems to be the modus operandi of the masses. In all likelihood, the first guy who made fire probably got punched in the nose by one of his fellow cave dwellers while being disgruntled about how this fire stuff was going to ruin everything.

It's a familiar story. Take electricity, or rather our ability to use it, is a fairly new technology, only becoming relatively widespread in the 1800s. Early in that century a movement called The Luddites arose. These guys were the artisans of the British textile industry and they created a social movement because they were terrified by the changes they saw coming with the Industrial Revolution. Looking into the future, they could see their jobs disappearing as looms became mechanized. In an effort to thwart that vision, they destroyed the power supplies that mechanized the electric powered looms as well as destroying the looms themselves. These Luddites protested the future not because they were stupid or even ignorant, but because they felt these changes would leave them without work and that would have created what seemed like dire consequences.

While they didn't succeed at preventing the mechanization of weaving, they did succeed in making their name famous, or perhaps infamous. The term Luddite is still used to describe anyone opposed to technological progress or technological change. We all know that there is no practical way of stopping progress. Whether you think that it's a good thing or a bad thing does not change the fact that progress and change are always coming. You can either stand in the way protesting and most likely get washed away in the process, or you can surf the wave of change to take you where you need to go in order to bring what you have to offer to the world. By the way, the individuals who see the change coming and prepare themselves or their industry for that change inevitably become very wealthy.

Now I am not saying that everything that is presented to us as "progress" is in fact good. We know for sure that much of that stuff has been an absolute disaster, and as a result we are clamoring to clean up our ecological mess; as Alan M. Eddison put it, "Modern technology owes ecology an apology." Technology has given you great advantages so what I'm challenging you to consider is whether or not you are being a Luddite. What part of technology do you need to stop fighting and start using in order to make better use of your efforts? How can you use technology to develop the goods and services that are the fruits of your unique value set? And then, how can you leverage technology to let people know what it is that you have to offer?

When I started out speaking and for a very long time afterwards, if you wanted to hear my presentation you had to either find a way to get yourself to a live event or find one of the rare stores that carried recording of my presentations. Today you can find my audios, videos, and books without leaving your living room.

You can read my ebooks.
(http://www.WhatTheBleepDoesItMean.com)
You can listen to my podcasts and teleseminars.
(http://www.DovBaron.Podomatic.com)
You can watch tons of my videos on YouTube,
(http://www.youtube.com/BMI2007) and many other places. You can even be on the other side of the world from me and get live video coaching and be part of a community of people who, just like you, are committed to personal growth and development.
(http://www.ResonanceCity.com)

What I want to point out here is whether you see technological advancement as something that frustrates the heck out of you or something you absolutely love, you are part of a system that leverages technology at every turn. And that, my friend, is one of the things you will need to do for yourself, if you want to truly create lasting wealth.

Let's say you just don't get it, and you just don't want to get it. You are not interested in learning the latest technology. Guess what? You don't have to learn it. You can leverage people.

Leveraging People

Despite what some people will tell you, leveraging people is not about subversively manipulating or conning people. It's all about finding people who love doing what you have absolutely no interest in. It's true. There are people out there who absolutely love doing the technical things you don't want to do and they would be willing to assist you in taking what you offer, applying the appropriate technology to it and, within a very short period of time, you will have a passive income.

As you are aware, this last couple of chapters has been set around creating passive-residual incomes. What modern technology allows us to do is develop systems and automate tasks that would normally take many hours to accomplish on our own in order to generate that passive-residual income. Today, with your home computer and a way to connect to the Internet, it is possible to set up an entire business online that runs mostly itself. As I said a few paragraphs back, you can get lots of my material without me actually having to directly do anything since the time I created those products.

You may not be the biggest, best techno geek but you probably know one who would be happy to assist you. Failing that, you can advertise on something like Craig's list or elance.com and be flooded with people to assist you within 24 hours of posting an ad. So, begin to think about how you can leverage technology to create a greater level of recognition of your own expertise and then use that to automatically start putting the greens in your jeans.

Passive income is created by using leverage. Money, time, people and technology, are all things that can be leveraged; this in turn multiplies not only your earning power but also their power exponentially and produces passive income.

Show Me the Excuse and I'll Show You Lack of Money!

The other excuse people use is "I don't have time." At the risk of up-setting some folks, I'm going to just spit it out—Bull Shit! It's easy to talk yourself out of an affluent state where you are generating a flow of abundance by saying that you don't have time. Listen, no one has time. We are all too busy to take something else on. So dump some-thing and then take on what you need to do. You know what? We are outside the nice zone and standing in the zone of truth so let me ask you to be absolutely bullshit free for a moment. How much time do you waste a week, or even a day? I know your ego-mind wants to say that it's not wasted time, that you need to chill out and watch your soaps or play that game or whatever else that distracts you from taking financial control of your life. You and I have been around all the law of attraction buzz, and the often magical thinking that goes with it. But if people really want to genuinely "attract" what they say they want, well then, there's going to be a need to address "the law of distraction" many people are actually running in their lives. Now just imagine what would happen if you put all the distractions off to the side and took thirty minutes a day to find a way to put your unique value set out there in the world? So what's stopping you?

For years I signed off my teleseminars by saying, "Time, money, en-ergy, and effort spent investing in the expression of your heart, soul and mind is time, money, energy, and effort well spent." I still whole-heartedly believe that. And that's exactly why I'm suggesting that you invest in yourself. By investing in each of those ways, you will come to recognize, appreciate, and own your value. Remember, your self-worth cannot be set by anyone else. However, the more you recognize and embrace it, the more you can share that value to the world. It's all about you recognizing and sharing your unique value. Self-worth is value expressed and that value is recession-proof.

"Learn to value yourself,
which means: to fight for your happiness"

~ *Ayn Rand*

As it turns out there has always been and always will be room for you at the top. Although those who cannot own their own value and as such cannot provide genuine value may rise to the top for a while; without value it becomes all about price. Those who compete on price alone fade from the limelight just as soon as someone can undercut them.

What about you? Are you willing to now start recognizing and embracing your value? Having gone through the exercises and discovered, or at least uncovered, some of the unique value you offer, you should know that the opportunity for you to move into both wealth consciousness and wealth experience is now. I'm not kidding. Most people will sit around and find friends to agree with them about why it can't be done but know this: Glory and living in affluence and abundance belong to those who are no longer willing to live lives of quiet desperation.

Remember, it's called passive income but that doesn't mean you can become passive about making it happen. You will have to be brave, do what it takes and find a way to take the massive action that will generate an abundant flow of cash.

Here's my sincere recommendation for you and it comes from the bottom of my heart. When you come across someone who already has what you want in life, and they give you an opportunity to buy their knowledge, experience, and lessons learned—DO IT! Remember what my buddy said about learning from my mistakes. It's always cheaper to find someone who has walked the path and can guide you around the potholes. I spend a reasonably large amount of money every year doing exactly what I have recommended you do—getting mentored. Mentors give you an opportunity to exchange money for their wisdom, knowledge, experience and maps of the minefield in the form of their books, audios, DVD's or private coaching, etc. I'm truly thankful for the opportunities to learn that I've had from each of my mentors.

The key is that once you have that passive income stream flowing, you can have the freedom to devote quality time to your family, volunteering for a worthy cause, or even in the creation of another new passive income stream. Or you could chose to just relax and enjoy life instead of having to work hard hour after hour to maintain it.

Leveraging Time
I started out this chapter talking about time and now we get back to it. As I said before, no matter how much you make an hour, there are only so many hours you can work. In order to move not just your wealth consciousness, but also your bank account in the upward direction, you must find ways to leverage your time.

The most common way to leverage time is to hire an employee to do the work for you that has a lesser financial value so that you can spend your time doing the things that have a greater financial value.

Now listen very carefully. I know that many people don't think they can afford to hire someone. However, very often that's not true when approached from a position of leveraging time. I have a friend who is a lawyer. We were chatting about where he saw his business going and he told me that he had recently added someone to his team. Even though he was excited about his company's growth, he told me that he was a little nervous at having to pay out an extra $40,000 a year for this person to be in his office. Trouble is, this guy's a lawyer;

he's a little smarter than the average bear but up until this point he had never thought about the concepts of passive-residual income or leveraging his time. (If you're not quite getting it yet, don't worry. You will.)

I asked my friend what his hourly rate was and he told me that he bills $350 an hour. I asked him if there were things he was doing in his workday that someone else with the right knowledge could do for a lot less per hour. He, not too surprisingly said, "Well yes, the person I was just telling you about could do many of the more menial things."

I asked him, "If this new person was doing this, as you called it, 'more menial' work. What would you be doing?" My friend quickly said he would be working on other files. To which I said, "And you'd be billing your clients for the work on these new files at $350 an hour, right?" "Yes, of course," he said looking rather bewildered.

"So while you're working on a new file, billing at $350, how much would this new person be billing out at for the work they were doing."

Still looking a little puzzled he said, "About half that."

"Okay," I said. "Let's do the math. Previously you would have been able to work on any given file and bill out for each of those hours at $350 and you would not have been able to work on anything else, is that correct?"

Still looking a bit puzzled my friend replied, "Yes."

"All right, now with this new person working on something and billing out at $175 an hour plus the $350 an hour you are billing which means you have $525 an hour coming in, is that correct?"

"Yes, but you forgot I still have to pay this new person."

I quickly replied, "Do you pay this new person $175 an hour?"

"Of course not!"

"Then the difference between what you bill a client for your new staff hours and what you pay them is profit, right?"

He got that, but what he had not yet realized was that as long as his new person was working on something, that freed him up to work on something else he could continue to bill at his full rate. It finally hit him that he had been doing work that he couldn't bill out at his full rate for, and essentially he had been robbing himself in the process.

In an effort to make this crystal clear, let me give you one more quick and very down to earth example. When my wife and I first got married, she was still working in dentistry. Even though her hourly rate of pay was pretty good, at the end of what was most often a very stressful workday she didn't have much energy left for anything else. At that time my business had changed direction and was really starting to take off. Saturday mornings would come around and we would get up, have breakfast, and start cleaning our place. We'd try to get it done as fast as we could and after about three hours with both of us really working at it, the place would be sparkling. One particular Saturday we got up after a pretty tough week of work and neither of us felt even slightly motivated to clean up. (Maybe you can relate to this!) We dragged our butts around the place doing a less than stellar job and instead of spending our remaining Saturday out and about we, very uncharacteristically vegged in front of the TV for the rest of the day. Suddenly I realized how crazy it was that we were spending our Saturday this way. I looked at my wife and said, "Let's add up what you make per hour to what I make and then times that by three."

Looking a little confused, she asked, "Okay, what's your point?"

"Do you think we could bring people in to clean our place for less than that?"

You see, it had just clicked that we weren't saving money cleaning the place ourselves. It was costing us more. I had realized that my hourly rate, plus my wife's hourly rate, times the three hours it was taking us to clean was a very expensive use of our time. The following week we interviewed different cleaning companies, and by the end of that week we were leveraging people; we found someone who genuinely enjoyed the cleaning work. And of course we were now leveraging our time, because the three hours we had each been spending cleaning, could now be invested in whatever we chose.

I am aware that most people get up in the morning to go to jobs they do not like. However, I want to share with you my central philosophy around money, wealth, and building a healthy economy. As I touched on a couple of chapters back; it's my contention that if we all got up in the morning to go to work in jobs we loved we would build a thriving economy. Even though that may sound more than a little idealistic, think of it this way: I don't enjoy tinkering with cars. I have absolutely no interest in lifting up the hood of my car to see how things work and even less interest in doing so with the aim of fixing something. In fact, if I tried to fix it there's a very good chance it would end up costing me more because I may have to hire someone to undo the mess I would most likely create. But you know what, surprise-surprise, there are people out there and maybe you're one of them who absolutely LOVE playing with and fixing cars. That being said, there are also people who fix cars for a living but hate every moment of their workday. My central economic philosophy is that I want to give my money to someone who absolutely loves doing whatever it is that I don't love doing. That way I am not only getting the very best work done, but energetically I am feeding into a loving workforce and a loving workforce would operate from a place of love and abundance as opposed to lack and anger.

The examples I just shared were examples of using local people with expertise to do what it would be more profitable for you not to do. However, websites like elance.com and many other on-line resources are available to help you find great non-local people to do the things you want done. One of the things you will discover about using these resources, and in honesty it takes a little patience, is that often the people live outside your own country. Again, we can fight the process, but the fact is that this is an outsourced world. What that means at the basic level is you don't need to have "an employee" doing the works. You can hire someone who is remote, meaning they are not in your office, (if you even have one). Meanwhile they can be thousands of miles away from you, answering your phone line, stating the name of your company, dealing with inquiries and even selling for you. They are private contractors and they will often do the work for a fraction of the price it would cost you to have them in your office.

Using these kinds of resources, Tim Ferriss, author of "The 4-Hour Work Week" shows us how he is able to live the lifestyle of what he refers to as the "new rich." As he puts it: ***Fun things happen when you earn dollars, live on pesos, and compensate in rupees.***

Listen, I'm not kidding around. I fully recommend that you look into finding someone to do whatever it is that you don't want to do or don't have the expertise to do. Now here's the important thing: You must then use that time to do something that will generate more income for you than whatever you are paying out. It's pretty simple but truly powerful, and it's something every wealthy person on the planet knows. I'd like to quote Tim Ferriss once again: *"The options are limitless, but each path begins with the same first step: replace assumptions."*

Put as simply as possible; you've got to be willing to drop your old ideas in order to get to where you want to go. The most important things you will ever do will rarely be the ones that used to be the most comfortable.

I told you that I grew up around people who were very poor. When we would see wealthy people having someone clean their car or do some other odd job for them, we'd say the wealthy person was "lazy," but you know what, we were dead wrong! The wealthy person was smart; they were leveraging their time. Look, **don't be a working class snob about this**. Find someone to do what you don't want to do, pay them the money, use the time to make more money for yourself and you will become part of a new collaborative economy!

Is this making senses? Or are you still battling against some old conditioning? If the idea of leveraging yourself to wealth seems like a bit of a stretch, I encourage you to read these sections over again, highlight, take notes, do the exercises, and talk about what you are learning with friends. Do what it takes to let yourself feel and know the power of leverage. The more ways you allow yourself to absorb this material, the better chance you have of retaining, using it and transforming your me-conomy.

The bottom line is that your true path to attracting, building, and keeping wealth is to continue to do what you would be naturally doing if you didn't have to drag your butt out of bed to earn an income doing something you could care less about. One of the key things about adopting an economic view that connects energy and money is that, by its very nature, it would put you around people who are interested in and fascinated by the same things that set your heart and soul on fire with passion. Being in that like-minded environment can be the difference between creative suffocation and creative blossoming. Please note that when you do this, you open up the possibility for others to see that they too can follow their passion and in the process make a wonderful income.

I'm trusting that this is now not only making senses, but light bulb moments are flashing in your head like a Fourth of July fireworks display.

Before we move on, I just want to present one more illustration of why you now need to fully embrace the power of leverage to put you in the flow of affluence. I realize that as you read this book you may already be a millionaire or even a multi millionaire. However, for now let's just pretend that you're not there yet. For a moment or two let's pretend that you are currently making between forty and fifty thousand dollars a year. I've come over and asked you if you want to take your income to that of a millionaire.

In this imaginary situation you reply a resounding "Yes!" I tell you that I have a very simple and totally legal strategy to guarantee that you become a millionaire one year from now. Do you think you'd be interested? Maybe a bit more than just interested? Good!

Then I ask, "Are willing to work a consistent fifty hours a week for a year?" "No problem" you reply because you are already working that many hours.

"Great, and are you willing to work fifty weeks of this year?" Again your reply is, "No problem" since you are already working at least that many weeks a year.

"Wonderful, then so far there are no challenges, right?" "Right!" You reply.

You can feel yourself holding your breath, just waiting for this millionaire solution. Very calmly I explain that by doing the prescribed amount of hours for the prescribed amount of weeks per year you can be a millionaire. That is, and here's where it get a bit tricky for most people, **as long as you charge $400 per hour**.

You must work each of those hours and be billing at no less than that amount. This means you cannot waste any time doing anything that is billable at anything less than $400 an hour. It's simple math. $400 per hour, times fifty hours a week totals $20,000 a week. Multiply that by fifty weeks a year and you get a grand total of one million dollars. Congratulations! You've made a million bucks!

This may seem impossible to you, but it isn't. Many people do it, year after year on a consistent basis. Most certainly, it is entirely possible if you begin applying what you have already learned here with regards to using leverage.

Is all this now starting to really make senses? To get to where you want to go, you will need to apply some form of leverage.

I have to tell you one last thing on leverage. How about leveraging brainpower? Find three or four other people like yourself, people who are committed to being in the flow of affluence and having an abundant cash flow situation. Meet with them on a regular basis to discuss how you can assist each other in leveraging your time, energy, effort, and technology. Maybe you'll be a little shocked to discover all the great things that can happen when you leverage brainpower.

Let's remember how we got here—by your looking at the unique value that you bring to the world. By focusing in on those things, you not only bring your attention to them, but also you begin to feed this recognition of your personal value into your QRF, expanding it exponentially. By virtue of feeding your QRF, you begin to attract more and more opportunities to express your unique talent, skill, or ability. Add to that the power of leverage and you have one of the great competitive edges that puts you in the flow of affluence and the circle of building wealth.

Chapter 27

It's Good to be the King/Queen

I don't know if you've noticed but not once in this book have I talked about setting goals in order to become wealthy. Having said that, I am in no way opposed to goals. In truth, we ritually have a process for setting them at the end of each year for the year to come. However, I've got to tell you, I have not seen any evidence to suggest that people postponing their joy until they've reached some external outcome is particularly effective.

It all comes down to this: Everything in my work is about you recognizing the value of who you are and what you uniquely bring to the world. Setting goals that are exclusively about getting something or being somewhere rarely, if ever, brings any kind of lasting satisfaction. Following the path of unique personal value is more about the constant development evolution and expression of that unique value.

I started out at the beginning of this book by saying that I hoped we were at the beginning of a fruitful and mutually beneficial relationship. As we move towards the close of this book, I'm going to trust that you have enough of a sense of me to know that I care enough to tell you the truth. Based on what you've read within these pages, is that a fair supposition? Okay, then it's time to address the elephant that may have been hiding in plain sight.

You may remember that very early on in this book I said: 99.9999 percent of people carry a deep fear of rejection? Well once again I feel it's important to reiterate that you must stay courageous in the face of rejection. Having once again brought the focus back to you embracing, evolving and expressing your unique value set, I want to point out that this means you will, to put it quite bluntly, as I've said before, piss some people off. You see there's a good chance that everyone you've surrounded yourself with believes whatever it was that you had believed. In fact, (this is where we begin addressing the elephant) if you ever want to really find out what you believed, take a look at your friends. There's a very good chance that they are the living, breathing manifestation of your old beliefs. When you stop believing what you used to, people will notice and even if they cheer you on initially, unless they also are committed to growth, you can be pretty certain that it won't take long before you bang into some major resistance.

I think that as much as we want to believe that those around us will support us in our growth, most of us have experienced, at least at some level, how threatening it can seem when someone starts to outgrow the group. It seems to me that because people don't want to feel the sting of rejection, all too often they will hide their changes, even the positive ones, as if they were shameful warts.

Let's imagine you've been really thinking about your unique value and you are starting to appreciate what you can offer and maybe you even begin to talk about it with some of your friends. Before you know it, someone says something so simple and yet so loaded— "You've changed!" If the fear of rejection has got you by the jugular, you'll likely say, "No, I haven't." What you are doing at that very moment is sending yourself a clear message that you'd rather have *their* approval than your own.

Stop for a moment and think about that, because if you let that sink in, it's not very pleasant; in fact, it kind of stinks! Hopefully that's a good thing because, maybe, just maybe, you'll stop pursuing the approval of those who can't see your value and instead give it to yourself. Until then, you can expect some people to feel almost betrayed that you are no longer willing to play the game of pretending to be a victim of rules related to having a boss in a "steady job."

You have to understand that at this point your QRF has shifted and that they may feel that shift as a direct threat upon them, at some level. You see, if someone in their field begins doing something else, then there is room for them to question their own reality. However, if they can get you to return to the old beliefs, the old reality, there's nothing to question. So if you don't pay attention to what's happening, there will be those who will do their best to try to pull you back into their resonance, their frequency, and their reality.

Many people have chosen to believe that they will never get anywhere in life because of that deep fear of rejection. If your family, friends, spouse, and those around you want to keep you down, even if they think they are doing it out of love, you need to find the strength and the courage to stand up and fight for what *you* want and what you need to express. You need to claim your divine right to live the life that you desire by expressing your own unique value and thus being in the flow of affluence.

Don't get me wrong. Your family and friends probably are well intentioned, at least in their minds. They are looking out for what they believe is the best for you. However, when it comes to taking advice and being mentored, I highly suggest that you find someone who has walked the path you are looking to walk and has done so with a lot of success. Advice from some well-intentioned person who knows nothing about the subject makes about as much sense as letting your mom remove your appendix with a with a pair of old hairdressing scissors she had in the drawer just because you love her.

Throughout the book I've encouraged you to reread sections over again, highlight, take notes, do the exercises, and I've suggested that you talk about what you are learning with friends. Having said that, it's also very important that you are discerning about what you share and with whom. Sometimes, and you likely have already had this experience, you'll share something with a friend or family member. They may be really excited and want to know more. Sometimes they won't show any big interest for a little while and then they'll come back to you wanting to know more once it's soaked in a little. Still others will give you nothing, and you've likely experienced this one too. It's as if you've hit an intellectual and emotional wall. And then there are the ones who will put you down, tell you you're crazy and ridicule you in no uncertain terms. That's why you must pay attention to the responses you are getting to what you are sharing. You know the old saying, *Don't throw pearls before swine*. Some people just won't get it; some people just don't want to get it, some people are happy that you got it, and some people will do everything they can to have you help them get it. You have to know who's who. Having said that, the more ways you allow yourself to get this material, the better chance you have of retaining, using it, and transforming your quantum resonance field, your life and your me-conomy to a place of affluence.

It may not be the most spiritually evolved moment of your life, but I can tell you that it's a pretty great feeling when those who ridiculed you are scratching their heads wondering how you did it as you drive by on your way to the celebration of your success. There's this wonderful line in an old Mel Brooks's movie called "The History of the World Part I" that I think is best suited to the moment I'm referring to: **"It's good to be the king."**

As we draw to the end of the book I would like to share with you the story of a man I have a lot of respect for because he did a lot more than read the books or gather the information. He lived them.

Despite the obvious challenges, Tony applied what I taught him and transformed not only his own life but also the lives of his loved ones. I want to share this with you because there's a good chance that you or someone you know is or has been where he is. Tony's story is one of much more than simple transformation of finances; it is a story of the transformation of every aspect of the man and his reality. This is a transformation that had nothing to do with, luck, fate or even destiny. No, Tony's transformation was a result of admitting what wasn't working, discovering what would work and then applying it without prejudice into every area of his life. His story deserves much more than a couple of pages toward the end of this book. However, I'm optimistic that you will be inspired by his true-life story and as a result, you too will take action and apply all that you've learned here.

Just one more thing...You'll notice that this story is all in first person. That's because it's not me telling you where he was or where he is; it's Tony sharing his story with you in his own words because he wanted you to know what's possible if you really want it.

Tony's Success Story

Before I had learned Dòv's Equation for Manifestation method to consciously attract wealth into my life, I had become a master at unconsciously repelling wealth from my life. The key word in that last sentence is unconsciously. When one is unconscious, one is oblivious to what they are doing right and what they are doing wrong. That was me. I didn't know what I didn't know. When I think back to that time of my life, that time of financial despair, with the knowledge I have acquired now it seems to all make sense. When I say that I don't mean just the poor financial decisions I made, but more importantly the poor beliefs and attitudes that led to those decisions.

A significant amount of my financial grief wasn't due to poor financial decisions but events which, at the time, appeared beyond my control. There were auto repairs, break-ins, theft, embezzlement of student loans, to name a few troubles. "Stuff" would just happen to me to make my already difficult situation (a young, then a single parent of two in my early twenties) worse. Every time I got some money in my wallet, an event would occur to take it away.

Despair and anger were the predominant feelings. Anger at others for putting me where I was. Looking back, my focus on where I was kept me there. The more I focused on my "situation" the more my situation was reinforced by "stuff" showing up. As my love for my children began to replace my anger and frustration, subtle changes began to occur for me financially. I needed to save money for a better place to live, a more suitable car, better food etc. Children are expensive. "Stuff" appeared a little less and opportunities opened up for me a little more.

What was the difference? Emotionally I had more love although anger and frustration were still there. I also began to focus more on where I needed to be rather than where I was. Although things were slowly improving, the changes were still unconscious. I didn't know what things I was doing right to improve my situation and I didn't know what things I was still doing wrong. Although the size of the financial pool was getting larger, I was still treading water. I had yet to know abundance.

After a number of failed business partnerships (which brought me subsistence not success), I went into the financial services industry as a financial advisor. (I am not ignorant of the irony here.) Even then, the first company wouldn't contract me after training me for four months and scoring the top marks in all the tests along the way. I had a previous bankruptcy, which I had disclosed at the beginning. There it was again, that feeling like I had been punched in the stomach. Four months of unpaid training all for nothing. By now, the unseen hands which felt like they had been pulling me under in the past had now moved to be pushing me down from above—a glass ceiling—that was how it felt. "Stuff" was happening in a different way, but it was still "stuff."

I was contracted by a different company and after my first year was introduced to Dòv Baron, his live events and the Equation for Manifestation technology. Once I became consciously aware of the mechanisms by which we create our own reality, I set out to reshape my life. In the four years since I began the process, I have made the shift from subsistence to abundance. For me it has become a lifestyle as I didn't just read a book or attend a workshop; I made permanent changes to the little things I do and think every single day.

For me being conscious and enjoying abundance is a lifestyle. I stopped referring to my ex in a negative way and complaining about my financial hardships or setbacks. I changed the language I used, the company I keep, the way I behaved, the way I expected to be treated, the way I treat myself. Some of these are big things to change, but so many of them are slight. When it comes to wealth, I have exchanged hope with expectation.

I started with manifesting smaller goals and with each success increased the scope and with it the expectation of success. I have incorporated the Equation for Manifestation technology as a daily routine into my life when I go for a walk into the woods near my house. I express gratitude for all of the abundance I have received and the abundance I am about to receive. There it is again—expectation. What is expectation to me? A belief based on certainty.

How have my views about money changed? Money is no longer the goal; it is merely the vehicle. As I write this, I am preparing to put an offer on a million dollar home (four years ago I struggled to pay $1000 in rent) and my parents with their paternal wisdom were telling me I have to cut spending here and there. In their mind for me to afford to finance purchasing a large home, I must cut expenses and save. STOP! I said to them. I don't need to shrink my expenses. I need to grow my income.

For me now, my income is not a finite quantity. I am not on a fixed salary, I leverage my time, the people I have working with me and the technology I need. Now that I am conscious to wealth attraction and how it works, some "stuff" still happens. How I feel about it and deal with it has changed. Deals fall in my lap, not out of it. Business flows to me. No amount of saving from my current situation would make a significant difference in financing the quantum leaps I have been making. Attracting new wealth is the answer, not clinging on to money with the false belief it is in short supply. Ironically, the more financial abundance I experience the less I desire material things.

Wow! What a story! I have to share with you that I'm so very proud of Tony. The guy is completely unrecognizable in every area of his life—from who he was to who he has become. What he only touched on is that as a result of the work he has done on himself, other lives have been enhanced. Through his work he has made many other people wealthy. Tony has on more than one occasion bought as many as 100 copies of one of my books to hand out to clients and friends. He does this because he wants others to have the kind of massive fulfilling success he has been able to experience because the underlying structure of how he does business is now based on being genuinely relational. As I said, many lives have been touched by Tony's willingness to deal with his crap and get out of his own way, not least of all the lives of his two children who he has been able to spend more quality time with and send them to different places in Europe for portions of their education. That's just a thin slice of the kind of transformation in this guy's life, and in truth, there are hundreds more stories that are equally miraculous, except they are not miracles. They are testaments to individuals like you who take what they learn and apply it in the face of difficulty and even ridicule.

Earlier in this book I said that **Genius Has Speed**. The truly successful, those who are living at the top of their game, do not have time or tolerance for those who want to bring them down. When a truly successful person encounters such an individual, they very quickly decide if this is a person they want to be around and, if so, just as quickly decide exactly how much time they can spend without this interaction having direct and negative impact. Remember, in order to help others you are required to help yourself first!

All right, it's that time; it's time to give yourself big congratulations for your investment in yourself. You took the time to read this book and that's a great step. Now please understand this, simply reading these words and remembering them is not enough. You may have done that in high school, but this is real life. Being able to quote what you've read to your friends and loved ones or strangers you meet isn't going to create the kind of change you are really looking for. Like Tony, you have to take action.

Tattoo this on your brain:

Knowing is one thing, doing is another!

So, the question is: **What are you going to do right now?**

Chapter 28

What if You're Broke
Compared to Where You Could Be?

All right it's that time, the end of the book and the beginning of a new affluent you. Well done. Aren't you proud of yourself? What? What do you mean by saying, "It's no big deal"? Actually it is. Remember what I told you earlier? The average person never reads past the first chapter of the books they buy. Now as far as I'm concerned, it doesn't matter how brilliant a person is, they're not going to get very far on only one chapter. So, please accept my congratulations for having made it all the way to the end of the book.

Now come with me as we take a look back and tie this all together. I want you to realize how much you've learned, but I want you to begin turning the knowledge in these pages into real affluence by living it, so I'm intentionally keeping this part brief. I encourage you to go back and re-read any of the sections that don't ring a loud and clear bell in your memory.

A Concise Review:

I started out talking about *The Interesting Idea of Money* in which we discussed the fact that money is nothing more than an idea. Then we looked at your level of *Unconscious Deserving*, which causes so many of us to give our value away.

Then we began our examination of the *False Set of Beliefs* about money you may be holding onto and why fear keeps people from reaching financial independence. I explained that getting a *Clear Focus* and learning to become a *Decision Maker* are major factors that divide those who are living in the full spectrum of wealth and abundance from those who are in a constant state of struggle.

We dug into understanding *How to Weigh the Risk Factor* for opportunities, based on alignment with your highest values. Then we looked at the metaphor of the abused *$100 Bill* where, I hope, you began to recognize and reclaim your own inherent value, as well as understand the *Difference between Self-esteem and Self-worth*.

That brought us to the understanding that the way you see the world in lack or abundance is because of the filters you have in place from the beliefs you hold in your head. I pointed out that Your Focus Is Your Reality and I asked you to be willing to open up to the fact that *We Live in an Abundant World*.

That's where we started our journey into how the latest *Quantum Research* is now proving what ancient spiritual teachings have shared for millennia. Remember that we are all connected not just to each other but to all things including all the money that is circulating this planet each and every day.

We learned that *Everything is Energy* including you, me and money.

From there we explored that *Feelings* of affluence, wealth, success and being in the flow and having a *Frequency Match* with money and wealth being attracted to you. We learned that the match between what you feel and what you get is called *Resonance*.

We then took some time to look at *Your Relationship with Money* to see if you might be pushing wealth, abundance, and affluence away because of your unconscious *Money Myths*. I asked you to look at what you need to *Forgive Yourself* for in order for you to see your value, and allow your worth to flow both to you and from you.

I then outlined for you the necessity of gratitude for moving out of that old lack mentality by explaining that *Gratitude Perpetuates Abundance and the Importance of Giving*. From there we got the understanding of how important it is to be *Specific about What You Want to Manifest* and how to make sure you aren't sending *Mixed Messages*.

Then I went even deeper into *How Resonance Works* and how you create your own *Quantum Resonance Field* (QRF). This naturally took us to you discovering a *Greater Clarity* about what it is that you want. We talked about how everyone who is wealthy has a highly developed *Wealth Consciousness* and how you can develop yours.

Next, we looked at the difference between *Having Money and Living an Abundant Life* and how you may have been guilty of *Telling Yourself Lies* by unquestioning and accepting other people's beliefs about *Working Hard or Getting a Good Education*. It was a natural flow from there to look at *How Do You Get More Money* coming to you, by recognizing and embracing your *Own Unique Value*.

As we neared the end, we entered into the possibly scary territory of the *Inevitability of Change*, people's natural resistance to that change and why *Your Dad's Job is Gone*. It was then a natural flow to discussing *Passive/Residual Income* as an important way to create and keep wealth as well as the *Importance of Leverage* with regards to money, time, technology, people, and even brain power.

Whew! We covered a lot of territory in these pages. I'm optimistic that you've found the stories I've told to be helpful and the information I'm sharing with you to be inspiring and actionable. The point of this, and all my work, is to help create a world in which each one of us understands that we have **A Divine Birthright** to live the life that we desire—a life which includes expressing our own unique values and living a rich and abundant life on every possible level—expressing our authentic power, passion, prosperity, and life purpose.

Will the knowledge I've shared with you throughout these pages work for you? Maybe, maybe not. A better question might be *will you work what you've learned into your life?*

As one of my business mentors Anurag Gupta puts it: "***There is no shortage of solutions. It's the implementation of those solutions that we are short on.***"

Whether you have agreed or disagreed with what I have shared with you within these pages, I trust that this knowledge has expanded your consciousness. Remember that the root meaning of the word ***affluence*** is "flowing towards" and so with what I've shared I have faith that this knowledge will allow a greater level of all that's good "flowing towards" you.

One thing to always consider when it comes to money and how we see it as part of our reality is this: No matter what you are theorizing about, whether it's things directly related to money or the things that seem to be completely separate, your theories are always going to be a reflection of your current economic state and your economic goals. Therefore, it's always worth considering the limitation and bias of either of these things.

You, my friend, now have a giant competitive edge, not that the focus was ever in having the edge over anyone else. No, more importantly you now have a competitive edge over where you were yesterday. You now have what it takes to build your financial wings and fly towards your highest potential carried on the winds of affluence.

Please remember to honor the truth of who you are and to know that there is only one you in this world and you deserve the best life has to offer. You have a unique value set that the world is waiting for and by not sharing it you not only rob yourself of its Devine expression, you also rob the world of the gifts it could bring others.

Thomas Edison said: "The people have an instinct, which tells them that something is wrong and that the wrong somehow centers in money."

From my perspective that "wrong that centers around money," is in not recognizing that what you have as a unique value set has worth. When you recognize your own worth, other people will too and be more than happy to pay you for that worth.

What if You're Broke Compared to Where You Could Be? And what if applying what you've learned here shifted everything in a flash and you began living in the affluent flow? So, I ask you: Will you come with me and climb the heights of affluence and abundant living that you are truly capable of?

This is Dov Baron signing off and saying that it's been an honor to share my years of study and research with you. Perhaps we will meet again someday in the pages of another book or preferably in person at one of my live events where we can look into each other's eyes, shake hands, hug and you will know that I'm on your team. Until then, I wish you every success in all of life's adventures and in your quest to building a truly abundant and wealth-filled life.

Live with courage....
Dov...
Giving you the competitive edge without losing your soul!

P.S. **What's The Plan, Stan?**

Remember, **I've given you a gift that for a limited time you can have two tickets to attend Claim Your Competitive Edge™ live event.** This is an event that **thousands of people before you have paid up to $1,600 per person to attend.**

You've read this book. The only question now is: **Are you ready to throw off the limitations and fears in order to go to the next level?**

You are....Great!

I've outlined the Claim Your Competitive Edge™ workshop as one of the most upbeat and lively experiential events you'll ever attend. At the same time, **the amount of knowledge and experience you'll gain at this event will propel you to new heights in your life, your relationships, and of course, your finances.** Claim Your Competitive Edge™ is immersive and experiential—you'll get to experience some of the most enlightening moments of your life and do things you never thought possible—things that will prove to you—**YOU ARE UNSTOPPABLE!**

Missing out on this event is like missing the juice of life itself!
I'll see you there.

Just go to: http://www.CYCEdge.com/drtmb

About the Author

Dóv Baron now serves as an advisor to corporate, creative and personal leaders around the world. He is a specialist in the psychology of leadership, peak performance, communication and the power of the mind. He is also recognized as the world's leading authority in the area of "Quantum Resonance Fields™" (QRF). QRF is the science of how our beliefs, emotions and thinking affect and sculpt every aspect of our lives. Another way to think of it is as the science of 'karma'.

As a renowned professional speaker, author, and television personality, Dóv is a man who lives with passion every day of his life.

He has risen to international prominence by delivering high energy, passionate, and often profoundly funny messages that guide his students away from mediocrity and push them to live up to their innate greatness, to become who they were born to be. This is a message Dóv has learned from overcoming the challenges of his own life, and one he is helping others apply to theirs.

Having traveled the world to study with Eastern and Western masters, Dóv brings the wisdom of the East and powerfully applies it to the practicalities of the West. He is a featured expert on television, radio and in newspapers.

Today Dōv conducts seminars, keynote speeches, and live training for leading companies and organizations. In 2002 Dōv wrote a dissertation on Personal Emotional Resonance Fields, the fields that determine and sculpt every aspect of our lives. Quantum Resonance Fields set the unconscious ceilings for our health, wealth, success, and even love.

Dōv's specialized knowledge is a highly in demand commodity. Through this work, Dōv is able to create the kind of shift that has taken companies to multiplying productivity and revenue far beyond their goals. Shifting an individual's Resonance Field changes not only one's income potential but also the quality of their relationships and joy in every area of life.

Dōv is an authority in understanding and stimulating human potential. Utilizing a powerful delivery and his ever-emerging insight, Dōv's customized presentations teach and inspire his listeners to innovative levels of accomplishment.

To find out more about Dōv Baron and Baron Mastery Institute go to http://www.BaronMasteryInstitute.com
Or, visit Dōv's blog: http://www.DovBaron.com

Tell Us What You Think

If you've enjoyed reading this book, I'd like to ask you to write down this number: 512- 827-0505, extention 1257

I've given you this number because I want to know what you got out of this book. You have my permission to call 512-827-0505, extension 1257.

Leave me a message and tell me what you got out of this book and what you are doing with what you learned. What are the results you have achieved by applying what you learned? The answers to these questions are very important to me, because I care about the impact my work is having.

I sincerely look forward to hearing your success stories!

Declaration of Financial Independence

When, in the course of human events, it become necessary for humanity to dissolve the limiting beliefs which have concerned them with their fractured past, and to assume among the powers of the universe, the unified and equal potentiality to which the laws of resonance and the quantum field entitle them, a decent respect to the opinions of mankind requires that we should declare the causes which sets us on this path.

We hold these truths as self-evident, that all people are created equal, that they are endowed by their creator with certain unalienable rights that among these are life, liberty and the pursuit of joyous prosperity. That to secure these rights, new mindsets are instituted, deriving their powers from the wealth conscious mind. That when any form of limiting belief becomes destructive to these ends, it is the right of the people to alter or abolish them, and to institute new empowering beliefs, laying their foundation on such principles and organizing their power in such form, as to them shall seem mostly likely to affect their prosperity and happiness. Prudence, indeed, will dictate that beliefs long established should not be changed for light and transient causes; and accordingly all experience hath shown that mankind are more disposed to suffer, while pains are tolerable, than to right themselves by abolishing the norms to which they are accustomed. But when a long train of mediocrity and failures begin to reduce them under absolute debilitating control, it is their right, it is their duty, to throw off such belief systems, and to provide new guards for their future security. Such has been the patient sufferance of the people; and such is now the necessity which propels them to alter their former belief systems. The history of human socialization is a history of repeated injures and usurpations, all having the direct purpose of the establishment of unacceptable limitations on the potential of these individuals. To prove this, let facts be submitted to a conscious world.

- We have been made to believe that our dreams matter not so much as our labor for wages and the payment of perpetual debt

- Our attention has been systematically diverted to matters of insignificant materialism and indiscriminate spending

- We have been conditioned to believe that our worth is equal to the opinions others have about us

- As a result our intrinsic confidence has been eroded by the subjective opinions of those in dissonance with us and our dreams

- Our natural instinctive reliance on strong relationships with one and other has been suppressed with contrived campaigns of terror and fear-mongering

- The constant bombardment of our senses with messages designed to manipulate, coerce and confuse us, threatens to keep us distracted, overwhelmed and fearful of taking action toward our true goals

We, therefore the representatives of a conscious humanity, in Resonant Congress, assembled, appealing to the creative force of the Universe for the clarity of our intentions, do, in the name, and by the authority of the good people of this planet, solemnly publish and declare, that these conscious souls are, and of right ought to be mentally and emotionally free and financially independent; that they are absolved from all alliance to the limiting beliefs of the past, and that all debilitating connection between them and the state of unconscious mediocrity, is and ought to be totally dissolved; and as free and independent beings, they have full power to engage wealth activating resonance, conclude personal growth, contract alliances, establish commerce, and to do all other acts and thing which independently wealthy people may of right do. And for the support of this declaration, with a firm reliance on the provision of divine guidance, we mutually pledge to each other our service, our good fortune and sacred honor.

Signed: _____

On This Day: _____